JOHN O. BRANCH is a successful businessman, father, grandfather and Vietnam veteran. John's belief system was severely challenged by two years of combat missions, including Operation Lion's Den, a great naval battle, which is honored in the U.S. Navy Museum. John's near-death experiences including a 45 caliber hollow point police bullet to the chest, have given him a unique perspective on life. Inappropriate medical treatment at the VA hospital in Portland, Oregon led to a three-year incarceration for a crime John did not commit. A plea bargain led to over two years in the Oregon State hospital. John is now enjoying his life and his family in a small town in Oregon.

"Normal is a setting for washing machines.
Happy Warriors are unique."

John O. Branch
www.johnobranch.com
john@johnobranch.com

The Warriors Guide To Happiness

John O. Branch

Published by Lion's Den Publishing, LLC
P.O. Box 1297 McMinnville, Oregon 97128
www.lionsdenpublishing.com

ISBN: 978-1-7355642-0-3

Printed in USA

Dedication

To all my peers who share my love for
the truth and long for freedom.

Acknowledgements

I gratefully acknowledge...
My little sister Lonnie and
my best friend Marty.
Thank you for coming to my rescue!
And my sons Jeremiah and Noah.
Thank you for your strength and your
love!

Table of Contents

Foreword

This account by John is not the first account by a combat veteran that I have encountered, but it is the most severe case of mismanaged treatment that I can remember. Finding the Lord through his trials is well chronicled and tied into scripture throughout his writing. This is a story that every combat veteran should read, if not for themselves, then for their brothers, who may be suffering from post- combat trauma. In my 26+ years in the military, followed by 20+ years in the ministry, I have seen the results, both good and bad. I have the utmost respect for this writer and applaud his bravery for exposing himself to reveal the real truth. . . God's Truth!

Jerry Keen, MCPO, USN (ret),
Vietnam Veteran

I Am

"I am the way, and the truth, and the life. No one comes to the Father except through me."

Jesus ESV
John 14:6

My life has been filled with many adventures. Two years of war in Vietnam, husband, father, grandfather, businessman, pilot, I am not those jobs, I am not those titles…

I am a Happy Warrior!

Chapter 1
The Best Day of My Life

God causes all things to work together
for good for those who love God, to those
who are called according to his purpose.
NASB Romans 8:28

I used to live in Dundee, Oregon. I
owned a beautiful home with an incredible view of the Willamette Valley. Every
Fourth of July I would sit on my deck and
watch the fireworks across the valley.
During the day I would sit on my deck
enjoying the view, hummingbirds would
fly around my head; I had many hummingbird feeders on my deck. I loved my
hummingbirds.

Sometimes, my grandkids and I would
watch Disney movies together and sing
songs on my karaoke machine.

Fifty-eight years old and living the American dream…at least that's what it looked like.

Over a decade had passed since I first received treatment at the VA hospital in Portland, Oregon. The VA had declared me permanently and totally disabled with chronic and severe PTSD.

Becoming a prisoner of war is what I feared the most during my two years in Vietnam.

My shipmates and I spent those two years fighting the North Vietnamese. Mostly nighttime raids.

Two years of being afraid had thoroughly screwed up my head. My belief system was a mess.

My spine was damaged and I needed surgery. The VA doctors did a great job except for one thing; they completely screwed up my medications. One of my doctors told me he was amazed that I survived the VA's mistake! The VA chemicals sent me into a total state of delirium.

Crazy as a loon, I ran away from the VA Hospital. The police had been notified but failed to locate and return me to the hospital. After several days I returned home.

I have no memory of that night. Recordings of 911 calls, Family and neighbor accounts are all I have to go by for reconstructing the Best Day of My Life.

Apparently about 1 o'clock in the morning my wife dialed 911 because I was completely insane.

Several police cars were racing to my house when I ran outside with a very large knife. I was screaming obscenities at Satan and stabbing the dirt...the inappropriate VA drugs had rendered my brain useless.

First on the scene was a police officer and his trainee. The trainee was instructed to stun me with the beanbag shotgun but was unable to pull the trigger. I can only imagine what was going through the minds of the two police officers as a crazy Vietnam veteran was walking towards them but not responding to their commands to stop.

The experienced police officer was now in a very difficult situation shoot to kill or_? He chose lethal force to protect the trainee. It's been almost 10 years now since that night, and I am very thankful for what happened.

The police officers did what they had to do... I would've probably done the same thing if I were in their shoes.

I do have a reoccurring dream, memory, or whatever it is. I'm standing in front of my house with a loose-fitting sweatshirt. No sound, just two headlights shining at me. Feeling something warm running down my belly, something like warm syrup. Then I realize... you shot me! you shot me! why did you shoot me? Then I fall to the ground.

I needed something horrible to happen to me. My belief system was a mess, and I was hopelessly addicted to VA drugs. It was a wonderful horrible experience… that 45 caliber hollow point bullet started me on my journey to happiness.

<u>Chapter 2</u>
Ideas

"The most dangerous ideas in a society are not the ones being argued, but the ones that are assumed."

C.S. Lewis

Assumptions followed me to war. Assumptions followed me home. Assumptions have caused me a great deal of suffering.

Happy Warriors are assumption-cautious.

Chapter 3
The Art of War

"If you know neither of yourself nor your enemy, you will never be victorious."
General Sun Tzu The Art of War.

"For our struggle is not against flesh and blood, but against the rulers, against the powers, against the world forces of this darkness, against the spiritual forces of wickedness in the heavenly places."
Apostle Paul NASB Ephesians 6:12

When I got back to the states from Vietnam I knew something was wrong. In the Navy I had purpose. My shipmates and I would work hard, fight hard, and play hard. This was not working for me in civilian life. I was unable to focus. My father and I founded a small business: the Corporation Branch and Sons. We both had dreams of making lots of money. My father and I would work hard and play hard. I would not drink until after work but after work I would really drink. Hard work and heavy drinking were no cure for my anxiety. I always thought that my anxiety was something that was being done to me by an external force. Blaming my anxiety on my circumstances, my work, my family, anything but my belief system. My belief system said you need to go back to being single, that's when you were happy. My love for my family was strong so I resisted. I decided to try and get rich. As a licensed real estate salesman my focus on money was easy. Everybody in my line of work was focused on money. I was surrounded by rich people and people that want to be rich.

My belief system was crumbling around me so I drank even more. Scotch lunch was normal. After work my colleagues and I would go to nightclubs and drink. I felt guilty but I kept drinking. Eventually my wife left me and took my son with her. I was miserable. My drinking increased. I hated getting divorced but my anxiety was driving me… *as a single Man I can be happy again*, I thought. Ignoring the truth, I decided to focus on my happiness. My belief system told me I was defective. The enemy was trying to destroy me.

Happy Warriors know themselves and their enemy.

Chapter 4
Belief Systems

"Everyone who hears these words of mine and acts on them may be compared to a wise man who built his house on the rock. And the rain fell, and the floods came, and the winds blew and slammed against that house; and yet it did not fall for it had been founded on the rock. Everyone who hears these words of mine and does not act on them will be like a foolish man who built his house on the sand. The rain fell and the floods came and the winds blew and slammed against that house; and it fell-and great was its fall."

Jesus NASB Matthew 7:24-27

Belief systems like germs, are hard to see, sometimes very destructive, sometimes alive and sometimes dead. Every human being has germs and belief systems. Some of my beliefs were good for me just like some of my germs, but some of my beliefs were toxic. The bullet that tore through my right lung and my liver marked the beginning of an incredible remodeling project.

My belief system at that time was in shambles. I needed something outside of myself - something painful - something horrible - something powerful to help me take the first bite. Belief system change, like eating a brontosaurus, starts with the first bite. I did not need to tear down my house I just needed to remodel… some of my beliefs were good some not so good, and some were killing me and my family. Foundation is crucial in any structure. The adventure that followed thoroughly tested my foundation.

Happy Warriors have the perfect foundation.

Chapter 5
The Cage

They promised them freedom, but they themselves are slaves of corruption. For whatever overcomes a person, to that he is enslaved.

ESV 2 Peter 2:19

I knew I was in for some serious pain when the doctor told me I didn't need pain medication anymore. The Jailhouse doctor was obviously punishing me. What the doctor did not know was that I had been falsely accused and it was not his job to judge anybody. The VA had me on a ridiculously high dose of opioids for a very long time. Years! This was really going to hurt!

Two weeks after back surgery, a 45-caliber bullet tore a hole through my chest. It had been only five days since I was gunned down in front of my home and now I was about to go through severe withdrawal. I knew this was going to be bad but I had no idea just how horrible. During withdrawal I wasn't sure what was real and what was not. My jailers locked me in a tiny cell by myself, concrete slab to sleep on, combination stainless steel sink and toilet, and very thick steel door with a little slot to slide food through. I was so sick I couldn't eat for a week. I could hear drunks and druggies screaming obscenities at themselves and others. Enduring all night rants from drug addicts and drunks, my withdrawal raged on.

Alone, in agony, my life in shambles, I reached out to the Creator of all that is and begged to die.

My jailers were kind to me but withdrawal was absolutely horrible. Migraines and back pain kept me in a cage.

Happy Warriors are free everywhere.

Chapter 6
Prisoner of War

Now when John heard in prison about the deeds of Christ, he sent word by his disciples and said to him, "Are you the one who is to come, or shall we look for another?" And Jesus answered them, "Go and tell John what you hear and see the blind received their sight and the lame walk, lepers are cleansed and the deaf hear, and the dead are raised up, and the poor have good news preached to them. And blessed is the one who is not offended by me."

ESV Matthew 11:2-6

There were a lot of things to be afraid of in Vietnam. Some of my shipmates were afraid of being in the water when it was on fire - that's what usually happens when tin cans get hit. I was afraid of being a prisoner of war… not just afraid, I was terrified of what the North Vietnamese and Chinese Communists would do to me if they caught me. Some of the guys joked about it, but I was actually horrified. I had heard a lot of stories about what the enemy would do to me if they caught me. Sure, I was able to pretend like the rest of the guys, but the constant stress of fear changed me. I was never captured by the Vietnamese but I was a prisoner of war for many years. My enemy has no power over me now.

Happy Warriors enjoy their freedom.

<u>Chapter 7</u>
Anxiety

Be anxious for nothing, but in every-thing by prayer and supplication with thanksgiving let your requests be made known to God. And the peace of God, which surpasses all comprehension, Will guard your hearts and your minds in Christ Jesus.

NASB Philippians 4:6-7

Six months in the Yamhill County Jail was miserable. Our clothing was thin T-shirt material. The food was horrible and there was not enough of it. Everybody loses weight in jail. Occasionally on H block guys from prison would stay with us. Curious about prison life and wanting to pass the time, I struck up a conversation with one of our temporary roommates. I learned a lot. He said prison clothing is a lot warmer and for their yard time they actually get to go outside. He said the food is not good in prison, but it was a lot better than jail food. I made a mental note about this because the district attorney was threatening me with 35 years in prison for the crime of attempted assault, a crime I had not committed. He also said that sometimes people are shot in the yard if they don't lay down when the siren goes off. I started thinking about what the food would be like in the mental hospital.

High anxiety was my companion the 12 days I spent in maximum-security at the Oregon State Hospital. I was rubbing shoulders with the criminally insane- murderers, rapists and kidnappers - you name it. My first night in maximum-security was truly special. Two good meals and a snack in my belly, I smiled as I slid between the nice clean sheets. The soft mattress felt so good on my back. I was all by myself in my own room with my own bathroom. Everything was so clean, and the staff was so nice to me. Then my joy turned to fear - I had no lock on my door. There were over a dozen criminally insane men just on the other side of my door, and I was going to have to go to sleep sometime.

Happy Warriors pray.

Chapter 8
I Am Not Defective

For all have sinned and fall short of the glory of God, being justified as a gift by His grace through the redemption which is in Christ Jesus.

NASB Romans 3:23-24

Everything about my stay in the Oregon State Hospital was telling me that I was defective. Chains on my hands and my feet to go to the dentist. My hands were actually chained to my waist... I was helpless. The dental hygienist caused me more pain than I have ever experienced in a dental chair. The dentist gave me a filling that fell out. I'm sure they were doing the best they could considering they were very afraid of me. I had been labeled mentally ill, PTSD. My peers and I all had labels.

We shared our labels with each other. The staff did not share their labels.

Titration off benzodiazepines was probably the most difficult thing I've ever done… no it actually was the most difficult thing I've ever done. Trapped in a mental hospital… titration causing confusion… days were very difficult… nights were worse. My two weeks in maximum security… did you get that? Two weeks in maximum-security at the mental hospital, surrounded by criminally insane people. Sure, I had my own room, but I could not lock my door from the inside. Every night I would go to sleep wondering if some crazy murderer was going to sneak into my room and do something horrible to me. Maximum security in the mental hospital. Where the staff was protected from the crazies by bulletproof glass.

After six months in the mental hospital I was completely drug-free! I felt so victorious I had done it. I was now completely free from the VA drugs. I was not anxious or depressed. I had my brain back, and every day I went to four hours of treatment mall - various group therapies. Did I mention that everything about my stay in the Oregon State Hospital was telling me I was defective? In hospital for over six months, drug free, model patient, they gave me a hearing, a release hearing. Witnesses showed up to say how afraid they were the night that I had gone crazy. My doctors could not find one thing wrong with me. My doctors recommended full discharge. The discharge panel told me I was appropriately placed here at the hospital. The powers that be informed me of my right to appeal, then told me I could ask for another hearing in six months. I said thank you. Staff took me back to my room. I could not believe what had just happened, my belief system was falling apart. I must be defective. I spent two more years with the criminally insane. During this time my belief system underwent remodeling. I am very fond of my peers. You see they are the only ones that truly understand me... I love my peers! As time went by the difference between staff and peers became more and more difficult to see.

Happy Warriors are unique.

Chapter 9
These Are Your Peers

"My brothers are these who hear the word of God and do it."

Jesus NASB Luke 8:21

Fifty-eight years old, incarcerated in a mental hospital surrounded by very heavily medicated adults. I was having some feelings. This is where I learned what the Thorazine shuffle is. I don't think that particular drug is actually used anymore but that's what the patients called it… the Thorazine shuffle. Patients so heavily medicated they struggle to walk. Staring at their feet, arms straight down to their side, shoulders slumped forward, they would slide. One foot a little bit forward then the other foot would slide just a little bit forward. I think you get the picture - they were really high. I have always been able to adapt quickly but this place… this place was something different. Heavily medicated convicted … murderers, rapists, kidnappers, so many violent and aggressive criminals. My new home was causing me a certain amount of anxiety. Security personnel were chaining my feet and my hands to my waist before taking me to medical appointments. Doctor appointments were on the Oregon State Hospital campus but I was considered high risk apparently. They would handcuff my hands to my side rendering me helpless. Then, and only then, they would take me to the doctor. You have not lived until you've been to the dentist with your hands chained to your waist. My first day at treatment mall was really something. Like being in kindergarten. Some of the classes provided coloring books and crayons. I had just survived six months in jail, virtually unscathed mentally and physically, but this was really starting to mess with my head. What really made the room spin was the statement made by one of the doctors. Standing in front of the group but staring at me, she said "these are your peers." I was speechless. Her words rang true. Is this what I've come to? Coloring books and crazies? I must be missing something… am I actually crazy and don't know it? I felt like a grenade had gone off in my head. This was the moment I began to examine my belief system.

Happy Warriors know who they are.

Chapter 10
The Battlefield

Whatever is true, whatever is honorable, whatever is just, whatever is pure, whatever is lovely, whatever is commendable, if there is any excellence, if there is anything worthy of praise, Think about these things.

ESV Philippians 4:8

God opposes the proud but gives grace to the humble. Submit yourselves therefore to God.

Resist the devil, and he will flee from you. Draw near to God, and he will draw near to you.

Cleanse your hands you sinners, and purify your hearts, you double minded.

ESV James 4:6-8

Maximum security in a mental hospital. How did I get here? There must've been two or three dozen patients locked up with me. We were in the new hospital. Everything was fresh and clean. Each and every patient in maximum security has their own bedroom with private bathroom. This is quite a change from jail where we shared toilets and shower. Seemed like about the same number of guys locked up with me. My new home was filled with the criminally insane. Wow... I did not feel safe. The ward office was behind bulletproof glass. This really did not make me feel better. The staff was great, even gave us a snack at night. My psychiatrist brought me many adventure novels to read. I was sure happy he ordered my medications to be dramatically reduced. Bedtime was special... no lock on my door, two or three dozen criminally insane men on my unit, I was not feeling very secure. Staff made rounds every hour through the night, but if one of the crazies decided to harm me....

Happy Warriors control their thoughts.

Chapter 11
Religion

"This people honors me with their lips, but their heart is far from me; in vain do they worship me, teaching as doctrines the commandments of men."

Jesus ESV Matthew 15:8-9

God made alive together with Him, having forgiven us all our trespasses, by canceling the record of debt that stood against us with its legal demands. This he set aside, nailing it to the cross. He disarmed the rulers and the authorities and put them to open shame, by triumphing over them in him. Therefore let no one pass judgment on you in questions of food and drink, or with regard to a festival or a new moon or a Sabbath. These are a shadow of the things to come, but the substance belongs to Christ. Let no one disqualify you, insisting on asceticism and worship of angels, going on in detail about visions, puffed up without reason by his sensuous mind, and not holding fast to the Head, from whom the whole body, nourished and knit together through its joints and ligaments, grows with the growth that is from God. If with Christ you died to the elemental spirits of the world, why, as if you were still alive in the world, do you submit to regulations-Do not handle, Do not taste, Do not touch (referring to things that all perish as they are used)-according to human precepts and teachings? These have indeed an appearance of wisdom in promoting self- made religion and asceticism and severity to the body, but they are of no value in stopping the indulgence of the flesh.

ESV Colossians 2:13-23

New Year's Eve, 1979 my wife and I were doing some last-minute shopping before going to several parties. I ran into an old friend from high school. We were all a little wild in high school, I'm pretty sure I got into more trouble than the others. We would compete in drag racing, illegal drag racing on the street. Anyway, I ran into this friend in the store. He said, "It has been nearly 10 years John what are you going to do tonight it's New Year's Eve?" "I'm going to get drunk," I said. He replied, "I'm sorry to hear that, John," My wife and I are going to do something different. We're going to church tonight and bring in the new year singing songs and playing guitars." My heart melted. This sounded so peaceful and he seemed so happy. That's when his wife and my wife showed up. We made our introductions and went our separate ways. My friend later reminded me that after he said he was sorry to hear me saying I was planning on getting drunk, I said "well I'm going to get moderately drunk." I had been suffering from high anxiety since Vietnam. I could not focus on work or family or anything. My drinking only made things worse. Trying to avoid thinking was impossible. That night my wife and I went to several parties, but nothing felt right that night. I did not get drunk but I did make a decision. New Year's Eve 1979 I decided to make some changes in my life. I decided to stop drinking and start reading the Bible and start going to church. I also decided to start praying every day. It has been over 40 years since that night and what an adventure it has been! Reading the Bible cover to cover with an open mind changed my life. I still read the Bible, and pray every day. I even go to church. Church is important for many reasons but the main reason for me is personal growth. Iron sharpens iron, so one man sharpens another. When I sharpen my knives, I notice little shavings. Tiny bits of my knife have to leave to be sharp. That's what happens to me when I attend church. Interaction with other people sharpens my belief system. We humans can be difficult to get along with, it's that interaction that helps me learn what I need to improve my belief system. The coming together of human beings can be a very good thing, it is also challenging. I have visited many churches over the years, and I never cease to be amazed at how the interaction with other humans sharpens me. There are many religious systems, and one thing is certain-humans are amazing! We have the ability to do great good and great evil. Over the years I've found it difficult to stay with one particular church; I value freedom and long for the truth. *Jesus said "the truth will set you free." Jesus also said "You can't serve God and money at the same time."* I am on a quest for truth. I have decided to follow Jesus.

Happy Warriors are not religious.

Chapter12
The Enemy

For our struggle is not against flesh and blood, but against the rulers, against the powers, against the world forces of this darkness, against the spiritual forces of wickedness in the heavenly places.

NASB Ephesians 6:12

Vietnam was my battlefield for two years. Victorious in battle, my shipmates and I returned home to face another enemy intent on our destruction. Guerilla warfare at home is relentless and brutal.

Happy Warriors know themselves and their enemy.

<u>Chapter 13</u>
Chain of Command

God opposes the proud but gives grace to the humble. Submit yourselves therefore to God. Resist the devil, and he will flee from you. Draw near to God, and he will draw near to you. Cleanse your hands you sinners, and purify your hearts, you double minded. Be wretched and mourn and weep. Let your laughter be turned into mourning and your joy to gloom. Humble yourselves before the Lord, and he will exalt you.

ESV James 4:6-10

The USS Providence CLG 6 was an impressive warship. Our weapons needed to be guarded day and night. I was 17 years old back then and rather impressed with myself carrying a loaded 45 caliber sidearm. After making my rounds I was required to report to the officer of the watch at the Quarterdeck. This was rather routine after a while; just a little speech I had to make standing at attention after a salute was returned. The Watch Commander was normally just a low- ranking officer. Didn't think much about reporting in until a senior Marine Corps Officer with a chest full of medals stood the watch. My knees were shaking and my voice was squeaking. He had mercy on me and I was allowed to live.

Happy Warriors respect the chain of command.

Chapter 14

Pastors

"I am the good Shepherd. The good Shepherd lays down his life for the sheep."

Jesus ESV John 10:11

"I am the good Shepherd. I know my own and my own know me."

Jesus ESV John 10-14

Occasionally my father would say interesting things. Actually, every day, interesting things were coming out of my father's mouth, even after he stopped drinking. One of his little sayings was "Pride goes before a fall." I think he was trying to tell me something.

I love dinner parties. One evening, a new friend and I were talking about TV shows, when she mentioned a documentary, sharing with me how fascinating it was. Thousands of people working very long days for free. They were followers. Every day their cult leader was paraded through the compound so that all followers could praise and adore him. Each day he would select one of the 90 some Rolls Royce automobiles.

Everything was being purchased with volunteer labor. Many bad things happened in and around the ranch, but these people continued to allow themselves to be taken advantage of until the organization was dismantled by authorities and the leaders thrown into prison. Many years later one of the followers, a Harvard trained attorney, was asked, "how could you possibly be duped into this?" His response was, "Pride. My pride. I thought I was too well educated and too smart to be tricked into anything."

Happy Warriors are careful who they follow.

Chapter 15
Put Your Own Oxygen Mask on First

A blind man cannot guide a blind man, can he? Will they not both fall into a pit? A pupil is not above his teacher; but everyone, after he has been fully trained, will be like his teacher.

Jesus NASB Luke 6:39-40

Why do you look at the spec that is in your brothers' eye, but do not notice the log that is in your own eye? Or how can you say to your brother, Brother, let me take out the spec that is in your eye, when you yourself do not see the log that is in your own eye? You hypocrite, first take the log out of your own eye, and then you will see clearly to take out the spec that is in your brother's eye.

Jesus NASB Luke 6:41-42

11 days after my 17th birthday I found myself on a commercial jet airliner heading for the Naval Training Center in San Diego, California. I was so excited. I felt so grown-up. I was in the Navy! In those days we were allowed to smoke on the plane, so I had a cigarette or two. Ashtray on each and every armrest; social norms certainly do change with the times. What a great day this was. Before the plane took off, the stewardess (that's what they used to call flight attendants) gave us the rundown on what to do in an emergency. The only thing I remember is put your own oxygen mask on first. This was counterintuitive to me. Shouldn't I be trying to help others first? The problem was if you don't have your oxygen mask on you are going to be useless.

Happy Warriors have excellent vision.

Chapter 16
I Am the Greatest!

"You know that those who are considered rulers of the Gentiles lord it over them, and their great ones exercise authority over them. But it shall not be so among you. But whoever would be great among you must be your servant, and whoever would be first among you must be slave of all. For even the Son of Man came not to be served but to serve, and to give his life as a ransom for many."

Jesus ESV Mark 10:42-45

I say to everyone among you not to think more highly of himself than he ought to think; but to think so as to have sound judgment, as God has allotted to each a measure of faith. For just as we have many members in one body and all the members do not have the same function, so we, who are many, are one body in Christ, and individually members of one another. Since we have gifts that differ according to the grace given to us, each of us is to exercise them accordingly.

NASB Romans 12:3-6

I am the greatest! I am the greatest! This was the chant of the young athlete. Even as a young man I knew there was something wrong with this. As time passed, as it always does, I watched this athlete grow old. No longer the greatest he eventually passed away. After my first wife left me, I was lost. My family gone, I had no purpose, I had no focus. My belief system encouraged me to drink-just like in the Navy. The alcohol just made things worse. Eventually my belief system was encouraging me to end it all. *You have no value, you are a failure at everything. The world would be better off without you. You are defective. Everything you touch turns to shit.* Another voice reminded me of the pain that I would cause my family. If I offed myself... I cried. My belief system was at war. Beliefs were telling me I had no value. Another belief was telling me to keep going. Some of my beliefs were actually lies; I was not a failure. There had been success in my life; the United States Navy had offered me a variable re-enlistment bonus. The Navy values me. They offered me enough money to buy a brand-new Corvette. Yes, I have made some very bad choices, but I still have value.

Happy Warriors know who they are.

Chapter 17
Freedom

"If you continue in my word, then you are truly disciples of Mine; and you will know the truth, and the truth will make you free."

Jesus NASB John 8:31

My belief system was so messedup... my body was starting to fall apart. My belief system was so defective; I was literally believing lies and destroying myself. My foundation was solid but the rest of my house needed remodeling. Hopelessly addicted to the VAcalm down pills, my clinician told me I would never be free of the psychotropic drugs.

I will be forever grateful to the police officer that chose lethal force. He is the one that sent me on the path to freedom. Happy Warriors walk in truth.

Chapter 18

The Great Mystery

God willed to make known what is the riches of the glory of this mystery among the Gentiles, which is Christ in you.

NASB Colossians 1:27

Anyone who does not have the Spirit of Christ does not belong to him. But if Christ is in you, although the body is dead because of sin, the Spirit is life because of righteousness. If the spirit of him who raised Jesus from the dead dwells in you, he who raised Christ Jesus from the dead will also give life to your mortal bodies through his Spirit who dwells in you.

ESV Romans 8:10-11

We were steaming between ports one night when I walked out on the main deck to have a smoke. Pitch black outside, the ocean was glowing, I thought I'd lost my mind. I discovered later it was a type of plankton that floats just under the surface and lights up when it's disturbed. It made more sense as I embraced this truth.

Happy Warriors embrace mystery.

Chapter 19
Like a Child

"Anyone who will not receive the kingdom of God like a little child will never enter it."

Jesus NIV Mark 10:15

"Whoever then humbles himself as this child, he is the greatest in the kingdom of heaven."

Jesus NASB Matthew 18:4

The Navy awarded me medals for my service in war. To receive honor, I first had to ask to be part of what the Navy was doing. I had to follow their rules not mine; I had to be trained.

Happy Warriors are humble.

<u>Chapter 20</u>
Wisdom

The fear of the Lord is the beginning of wisdom, and the knowledge of the Holy One is understanding.

NASB Proverbs 9:10

The wisdom from above is first pure, then peaceable, gentle, reasonable, full of mercy and good fruits, unwavering without hypocrisy.

NASB James 3:17

If any of you lacks wisdom, let him ask God, who gives generously to all without reproach, and it will be given him. But let him ask in faith, with no doubting, for the one who doubts is like a wave of the Sea that is driven and tossed by the wind. For that person must not suppose that he will receive anything from the Lord; he is a double minded man, unstable in all his ways.

ESV James 1:5-8

Some of the happiest times in my life were my John O. Branch Chimney Sweep days. People, places, and situations were constantly changing and the money was good. The constantly changing part helped me to ignore certain beliefs.

I was at the top of a tall chimney when I noticed something was wrong; the chimney was moving. I had cleaned thousands of chimneys, and none of them had ever done this. Pushing away from the chimney, I fell to the roof. The weight of the very old brick chimney hitting the roof sounded like high explosives. My assistant helped me get down. Later, my doctor told me he was going to have to cut off my leg. I had just been informed that I was going to lose my leg and all I could think of was how am I going to climb ladders now? I decided to negotiate. A few days later I left the hospital with both legs.

I'm an old man now, piecing together fragments of my life. I think I understand what my friend was trying to tell me. "John, knowing the wood stove is hot is knowledge, not touching it is wisdom."

Happy Warriors seek wisdom.

Chapter 21
The Way

"I am the way, and the truth, and the life; no one comes to the Father but through me.

Jesus NASB John 14:6

One of my earliest memories is a fishing trip. My father had a fiberglass boat that was too small for the ocean but my Dad and one of his friends decided to take their sons across the Columbia River bar to fish for salmon. I don't remember exactly how old I was; probably around seven. The Columbia River bar is treacherous. I don't know what my father was thinking, but away we went. That day we were all in grave danger. The waves were huge and the boat was tiny. Crossing the bar going into the Pacific went okay. It was the return that was terrible. Nobody told me to reel in my line, which is the normal thing to do before going back across the bar, so I was able to see my bait, herring on a double hook, pop out of the top of a huge wave that was towering over the back of our boat. We made it safely back to the dock. My father and his friend were doing a lot of drinking and laughing. I think they were trying to pretend they had not been afraid. The Columbia River bar has claimed the lives of many a sailor. Large ships are required to have a special guide; I believe they are called harbor pilots or something like that, but they definitely know what they are doing.

Happy Warriors know the way.

Chapter 22
Milk

Putting aside all malice and all deceit and hypocrisy and envy and all slander, like newborn babies, long for the pure milk of the word, so that by it you may grow in respect to salvation, if you have tasted the kindness of the Lord.

NASB 1 Peter 2:1-3

You have come to need milk and not solid food. For everyone who partakes only of milk is not accustomed to the word of righteousness, for he is an infant. But solid food is for the mature, who because of practice have their senses trained to discern Good and Evil.

NASB Hebrews 5:12-14

Lunchtime was fun time at Llewellyn grade school. My friends and I were always up to something. We could always count on little cartons of milk being sold for two pennies, at least that's what I remember. Craving attention one day, I decided to impress my friends with my ability to drink many cartons of milk. Sort of a grade school chugging contest with only one needy contestant. My friends praised me for my milk chugging prowess and I soon learned a very good life lesson; peer admiration is not enough compensation for self-inflicted flu.

Happy Warriors know what's good for them.

Chapter 23
Rules of Engagement

Take the helmet of salvation, and the sword of the Spirit, which is the word of God, praying at all times in the spirit, with all prayer and supplication. To that end, keep alert with all perseverance.

ESV Ephesians 6:17-18

In Vietnam I knew I was at war. I knew I was in danger. Even the ocean wanted to kill and eat me. I thought when I was able to go home, war would be over, War is never over.

Happy Warriors fight.

<u>Chapter 24</u>
Knowledge

The mind of the intelligent seeks knowledge, but the mouth of fools feeds on folly.

NASB Proverbs 15:14

Better is a little with the fear of the Lord than great treasure and turmoil with it.

NASB Proverbs 15:16

Knowledge is knowing the fire is hot... wisdom is not touching it.

Happy Warriors seek Knowledge and Wisdom.

Chapter 25
Sea Snakes

Be careful how you walk, not as unwise men but as wise, making the most of your time, because the days are evil.
Ephesians 5:15-16 NASB

Snakes in the ocean, Who would've thought? These things are extremely poisonous, We were warned about the deadly snakes every time we got close to Vietnamese waters. Occasionally I would see hundreds of them entangled with each other. Very creepy.

Happy Warriors are cautious.

Chapter 26
The VA Hospital

There was a woman who had had a discharge of blood for 12 years, and who had suffered much under many physicians, and had spent all that she had, and was no better but rather grew worse.

ESV Mark 5:25-26

Doctors had been unable to discover the cause of my migraine headaches and stroke-like symptoms. My life was completely falling apart because I was unable to function. Late one night when I was having an extremely bad episode, a good friend of mine, a retired deputy sheriff and fellow veteran, came to my house. My friend began his sales pitch. "John I've been going to the VA and they do a real good job for me." In pain and desperate, I gave up and went to the one place I was terrified of, the VA hospital.

Everything, and I mean everything, got worse.

Happy Warriors are careful who they trust.

Chapter 27
The 11th Commandment

"You shall love the Lord your God with all your heart and with all your soul and with all your mind. This is the great and first Commandment. And a second is like it: You shall Love your neighbor as yourself."

Jesus ESV Matthew 22:37-39

After I had sons of my own, my father said "John, when you were just a little guy, I took you fishing. On the way home in the pickup truck you were so happy that you stood on the seat and kissed me on the cheek repeatedly." That is the kind of love I want for myself and others.

Happy Warriors love themselves.

Chapter 28
Do you want to get well?

When Jesus saw him lying there, and knew that he had already been a long time in that condition, He said to him, "Do you wish to get well?"

Jesus NASB John 5:6

One definition of insanity is keep doing the same thing over and over again expecting a different result.

The VA labeled me with PTSD and began drug therapy. Year after year I kept getting worse.

The question I should've asked myself was. *Do you want to get well?*

Happy Warriors want to be well.

Chapter 29
Life

"I am the resurrection and the life; he who believes in Me will live even if he dies, and everyone who lives and believes in Me will never die. Do you believe this?"
Jesus NASB John 11:25-26

Often my pride has gotten in the way of my happiness. The cage definitely called attention to flaws in my belief system.

My belief system has always had a solid foundation. Everything above the foundation, however, has undergone extensive remodeling.

Happy Warriors are teachable.

Chapter 30
Thirsty

"I am the bread of life; whoever comes to Me will not hunger, and whoever believes in Me will never thirst."

Jesus NASB John 6:35

"Blessed are those who hunger and thirst for righteousness, for they shall be satisfied."

Jesus ESV Matthew 5:6

The mental hospital had rules for everything. The food was healthy but it was also highly regulated. No second servings of anything except the salad. One small carton of milk per meal per person. Breakfast was the one exception; you could have a second milk at breakfast. Overall the chow was okay. Similar to military chow, only with portion limitations. Often my peers and I would talk about food…food and freedom. Oatmeal was a popular breakfast food served only occasionally. Often the oatmeal would run out, disappointing the last people in line. The oatmeal was being dished out by a server; however, this never stopped the server from blaming the last person receiving oatmeal. I found that interesting. I was new to the hospital and decided to advocate for the patients. Well, for the patients and myself, but mostly for myself, because of the oatmeal shortage. I decided to let the milk issue go. I believe that was the time I learned my lesson about the dangers of patient advocacy. My attempts to Improve conditions brought hostility down on me and changed nothing. One of my peers shrugged his shoulders and said "it is what it is." He had been in the hospital almost 5 years and already learned his lessons.

Happy Warriors eat and drink well.

Chapter 31
Light

"I am the light of the world. Whoever follows me will not walk in darkness, but will have the light of life."

Jesus ESV John 8:12

Flashlights have always held a special place in my heart. When I was about four years old my little sister and I would make a tent out of blankets and read comic books in the dark with flashlights. Such a perfect memory!

Happy Warriors use all the weapons of war.

Chapter 32

Green Eyes

"Truly, truly, I say to you, unless one is born again he cannot see the kingdom of God."

Jesus NASB John 3:3

"Try these, Branch." My shipmate handed me something I had never seen before. "Put them on" he barked. We were running lights out off the coast of Vietnam. Midnight and no moon made it impossible to see anything on the water.

Putting my ball cap in my back pocket I slipped the strap over my head and pulled the device over my eyes. "Everything is green" I said." Yeah we can see in the dark with these things."
I had no idea this was possible!

Happy Warriors know what it takes to see.

<u>Chapter 33</u>
The Wind

"Do not marvel that I said to you, you must be born again. The wind blows where it wishes, and you hear its sound, but you do not know where it comes from or where it goes. So it is with everyone who is born of the spirit."

Jesus ESV John 3:7-8

My peers at the Oregon State Hospital were tormented by forces seen and unseen. I developed a great sense of admiration for my peers who, in spite of horrible pain, would keep searching for the truth.

Happy Warriors know how to look.

<u>Chapter 34</u>
I Am

"I am the way, and the truth, and the life. No one comes to the Father except through me."

Jesus ESV John 14:6

My life has been filled with many adventures. Two years of war in Vietnam, husband, father, grandfather, businessman, pilot, I am not those jobs, I am not those titles...

I am a Happy Warrior!

Chapter 35
Direction

I will instruct you and teach you in the way you should go; I will counsel you with my eye upon you.

ESV Psalm 32:8

Construction sites are very dangerous places. My father was a brick and stone mason. I enjoyed working for my Dad. The work of a hod carrier Is difficult and dangerous but my father taught me well, always keeping an eye on me.

Happy Warriors are teachable.

<u>Chapter 36</u>
Iron Sharpens Iron

Iron sharpens iron, so one man sharpens another.

NASB Proverbs 27:17

My shipmates and I carried knives. To be useful a knife needs to be sharp. I would use a stone to sharpen my knife. Carefully rubbing the knife edge against the other surface. My knife and the stone would change in the process. Barely noticeable, little bits of material would come off both the knife and the stone in the sharpening process. During a time of tremendous stress in my life I reached out to an old friend of mine. Excited that he had called me back I asked him about his life. He shared. I needed someone to listen. But my friend was too busy, his wife calling him to dinner. He told me he would call me again in a few weeks. I felt hurt. He often seemed to condescend to me… like he was doing me a big favor by talking to me. I was enraged by his insults. Angry for several hours, I considered going back to some old ways. Then I remembered the words of Jesus, "turn the other cheek." Also, from the Bible, "never return evil for evil." Then I remembered the words of one of my friends: "John, just because someone hands you a stick you don't have to keep hitting yourself with it." I took action on the truth and started praying for my friend. He was probably unaware of the pain he had caused me. I find it impossible to hate someone when I am praying for them. I'm sure my prayer helped me more than him because I felt peace and joy. My anger was gone. And I am a little bit sharper.

Happy Warriors value training.

Chapter 37
Voices

I told you, and you do not believe; the works that I do in my Father's name, these testify of Me.

But you do not believe because you are not of My sheep. My sheep hear My voice, and I know them, and they follow Me, and I give eternal life to them, and they will never perish; and no one will snatch them out of my hand. My Father, who has given them to Me, is greater than all; and no one is able to snatch them out of the Father's hand. I and the father are one.

Jesus NASB John 10:25-30

And when Jesus had stepped out of the boat, immediately there met him out of the tombs a man with an unclean spirit. He lived among the tombs. And no one could bind him anymore, not even with a chain, for he had often been bound with shackles and chains, he wrenched the chains apart, and he broke the shackles in pieces. No one had the strength to subdue him.

Night and day among the tombs and on the mountains he was always crying out and cutting himself with stones. And when he saw Jesus from afar, he ran and fell down before him. And crying out with a loud voice, he said, "what have you to do with me, Jesus, son of the most-high God? I adjure you by God, do not torment me." For he was saying to him, "come out of the man, you unclean spirit!" And Jesus asked him, "what is your name?" He replied, "my name is Legion for we are many."

ESV Mark 5:2-9

A very long time ago a friend of mine said you cannot stop birds from flying but you can stop them from building nests in your hair.

"My name is Legion for we are many."
Happy Warriors know who to listen to.

Chapter 38
Time

When they had rowed about three or 4 miles, they saw Jesus walking on the sea and coming near the boat, and they were frightened. But he said to them, "It is I, do not be afraid." Then they were glad to take him into the boat, and immediately the boat was at the land to which they were going.

ESV John 6:19-21

My grandmother told me, "Time is different when you get old."

Dozens of my peers and staff at the Oregon State Hospital told me I should write a book about my experiences. Everybody enjoyed hearing the story about how I got shot in the chest. Another one of my favorites is when I walked into Cell Block H. Everybody staring at me. After a few hours one of the gangbangers approached me. Tattoos everywhere. Head, face, neck… I mean everywhere. The gangster asked me, "are you the one that was on TV?" I lifted up my T-shirt, pulled the bandage off, and showed him the hole in my chest. He was very impressed. I now had street credit. Among the incarcerated I had status.

New experiences and new friends have always been important to me. People give my life meaning, sharing my story is good for me.

It's been many years since I started my book. I have started and stopped many times. The pain of my past too much to handle. Time passes slowly when I focus on the past.

Happy Warriors focus on Jesus.

Chapter 39
Don't Look Down

Peter said to Him, "Lord, if it is You, command me to come to You on the water." And He said, "Come!" And Peter got out of the boat, and walked on the water and came toward Jesus. But seeing the wind, he became frightened, and beginning to sink, he cried out, "Lord save me!" Immediately Jesus stretched out his hand and took hold of him and said to him "You of little faith, why did you doubt?"

NASB Matthew 14:28-31

Occasionally my father would share interesting words of wisdom. "When you are ass deep in alligators it's easy to forget that your goal was to drain the swamp."

Focusing on problems never ends well for me.

Happy Warriors focus on Jesus.

Chapter 40
The Door

I am the door; if anyone enters through Me, he will be saved, and will go in and out and find pasture.

Jesus NASB John 10:9

Watertight doors aboard Navy ships are much different than the doors in our homes. Water tight doors aboard navy ships are designed to keep sailors alive. Special training is necessary to operate these doors. Access to the gun fire control director was not intuitive, I had to have special training. I needed special training so I could go in and out of the door to access my battle station. My life and the life of my shipmates depended on me using the door.

Happy Warriors use the door.

Chapter 41
The Sword of the Spirit

Our struggle is not against flesh and blood, but against the rulers, against the powers, against the world forces of this darkness, against the spiritual forces of wickedness in the heavenly places.

NASB Ephesians 6 :12

And take the helmet of salvation, and the sword of the Spirit, which is the word of God.

NASB Ephesians 6:17

The United States Navy spent a great deal of time and money training me to destroy an enemy I could see with my eyes. During my first firefight in Vietnam I realized how real the enemy was. They were actually trying to kill me… this was real! These people hate me and want to destroy me. While I was fighting an enemy, I could see with my eyes another enemy was trying to destroy me. A much more powerful enemy I could not see with my eyes. This invisible enemy was trying to destroy me from within.

Using much different weaponry; Lies, deception, and misdirection his favorite tools. This invisible enemy was attacking my very soul. This enemy had penetrated my outer perimeter. My enemy followed me home working hard to corrupt my dreams and destroy those I loved.

Happy Warriors use their weapons.

Chapter 42
Self-Righteousness

Every man's way is right in his own eyes, But the Lord weighs the hearts.
NASB Proverbs 21:2

My group facilitator's words; "These are your peers" penetrated my protective armor. Facing the truth made my head spin. These crazy people really are my peers! I must be crazy too! My whole world was spinning. Is this how crazy people think? Do all crazy people think that they are normal. How did I get here?

The next year was spent analyzing reality. I read everything I could get my hands on. Cover to cover, I read the Bible, Quran, the AA big book, many novels, and self-help books.

Titration off all psychotropic medications brought reality into clear focus. My love for my peers grew and grew. Eventually I could see only one difference between staff and peers; the staff got to go home after their shift. I miss the honest sharing of Truth with my peers. I am ashamed to admit it now, but upon arrival at the Oregon State Hospital I felt superior to my peers. How could I have been so blind? Thinking that I was superior to anybody is crazy!

Happy Warriors are no better than anybody else.

Chapter 43
Labels

Then he went home, and the crowd gathered again, so that they could not even eat. And when his family heard it, they went out to seize him, they were saying, "He is out of his mind."

Jesus ESV Mark 3:21

The Oregon State Hospital helped me to see that all humans are crazy.

Happy Warriors are unique.

Chapter 44
Revenge

See that no one repays anyone evil for evil, but always seek to do good to one another and to everyone, give thanks in all circumstances; for this is the will of God in Christ Jesus for you. Do not quench the Spirit.

ESV 1 Thessalonians 5:15-19

"Love your enemies and pray for those who persecute you."

Jesus ESV Matthew 5:44

Dress blues and medals, one last time. I thought, "this will be nice." When my wife picks me up at the airport, maybe get a picture. Yeah, this is a good day; I will be free and home, and nobody is shooting at me. Taking my seat next to a young businessman, my day began to take an ugly turn. The self-righteous young businessman began to verbally abuse me for going to Vietnam. I immediately went into full combat mode. Neutralize the threat, destroy the target. We made it safe and sound to Portland, Oregon. I chose to not speak the entire trip. He never knew just how close he came to death that day. My hatred boiled inside me. For many years I hated him and all the others that had wronged me. My hatred was like a knife... always handy... always available to cut myself with.

Happy Warriors do not cut themselves.

Chapter 45
Choices

"No one can serve two masters; for either he will hate the one and love the other; or he will be devoted to one and despise the other. You cannot serve God and wealth."

Jesus NASB Matthew 6:24

John O. Branch Chimney Sweep was by far my favorite business. I thoroughly enjoyed my work and my customers. My family was also happy. I was focused on doing the right thing every day. Every morning, while my work van was warming up, I would say a little prayer:

"Heavenly Father, please help me to do perfect work today and please help my customers to know that I am doing the best job possible for them. In Jesus name I ask this, Amen." I was focused on doing the right thing. I knew if I did the right thing the money would follow.

Happy Warriors serve their commander.

Chapter 46
Suffering

Humble yourselves under the mighty hand of God, that he may exalt you at the proper time, casting all your anxiety on Him, because He cares for you. Be of sober spirit, be on the alert. Your adversary, the devil, prowls around like a roaring lion, seeking someone to devour. But resist him, firm in your faith, knowing that the same experiences of suffering are being accomplished by your brethren who are in the world. After you have suffered for a little while, the God of all grace, who called you to His eternal glory in Christ, will Himself perfect, confirm, strengthen and establish you. To him be dominion forever and ever. Amen

NASB 1 Peter 5:6-11

High anxiety was my companion for a very long time. Everything I did was intense. Over-work, over-play, over-drink, over-exercise, intensity is how I dealt with anxiety. By the time I reached my late 40s, my body was falling apart. Overdoing everything was killing me, but that was my way. VA drugs were useless. Finally, the inappropriate VA drugs put me into a temporary state of delirium. Three years in the cage gave me time to think. My years at the Oregon State Hospital were wonderful and horrible.

Conversations with my peers made the differences between normals and peers fade away. The cage helped me to realize pride had been keeping happiness at bay. Happy Warriors know their limitations.

Chapter 47
Forgiveness

"Do not be like them; for your father knows what you need before you ask him. Pray, then, in this way: our father who is in heaven, Hallowed be Your name. Your kingdom come, Your will be done. On earth as it is in heaven. Give us this day our daily bread and forgive us our debts as we also have forgiven our debtors. And do not lead us into temptation but deliver us from evil."

Jesus NASB Matthew 6:8-13

"For if you forgive others their transgressions, your heavenly father will also forgive you. But if you do not forgive others, then your father will not forgive your transgressions."

Jesus ESV Matthew 6:14-15

Every veteran is given a parting gift along with his discharge papers. Mine was unforgiveness.

For many years I drug my gift behind me like a rotting corpse. Unforgiveness was the scourge I beat myself with.

Eleven days after my 17th birthday the United States Navy began training me to be a sailor. This was a wonderful time in my life. I was doing a man's work, receiving a man's paycheck. I felt so grown-up! On the days that we did well in bootcamp, our Chief would let us smoke cigarettes. Never dreamed I could do so many push-ups and jumping jacks, but the United States Navy knows how to get young people in shape. My recruiter had promised me helicopter mechanic training. I loved working on cars and motorcycles, and had studied auto mechanics at Portland Community College. Basic training nearly complete, I could hardly wait for my orders. Helicopter mechanic training was going to be a breeze. Pulling my orders from a large manila envelope my heart was filled with joy and anticipation. As I read my orders a sick feeling of confusion filled my soul. The Navy was sending me to FT School. My recruiter had promised me helicopter mechanic school. I couldn't believe my eyes. The Navy had lied to me. The Navy had betrayed me, and so I chose to hate them.

The Navy flew me to Bainbridge Maryland where I studied mathematics and electronics.

FTG…fire control technician guns. FTG's aim the navy guns, the big guns.

The Navy had me over a barrel, and there was nothing I could do. Well, there was one thing I could do, not give them 100%, and that's exactly what I chose to do. I decided to do poorly, but just well enough to pass. That's how I would punish them.

Heavy drinking became my new life-style. I sure showed them, I finished last in my class.

Unforgiveness, the gift that keeps on giving.

Happy Warriors forgive themselves and others.

Chapter 48

Hope

Let us be sober, having put on the breast plate of faith and love, and as a helmet, the hope of salvation.

NASB 1 Thessalonians 5:8

War was difficult for me. No matter how difficult times were I always knew that eventually my enlistment would end and I could go home.

Happy Warriors hope.

<u>Chapter 49</u>
Why?

"Rabbi, who sinned, this man or his parents, that he was born blind?" Jesus answered, " It was not that this man sinned, or his parents, but that the works of God might be displayed in him."

ESV John 9:2-3

That evening at sundown they brought to him all who were sick or oppressed by demons. And the whole city was gathered together at the door. And he healed many who were sick with various diseases, and cast out many demons. And he would not permit the demons to speak, because they knew him.

ESV Mark 1:32-34

My choices have been the root cause of much of my life's suffering, but not all.

Happy Warriors make good choices, but still suffer.

Chapter 50
Creation

What can be known about God is plain to them, because God has shown it to them. For his invisible attributes, namely, his eternal power and divine nature, have been clearly perceived, ever since the creation of the world, and the things that have been made. So they are without excuse.

ESV Romans 1:19-20

"I don't want to believe that." said my peer. The Oregon State Hospital was one of the most difficult and challenging experiences of my life. However, there are a few things I do miss about the mental hospital. Conversations with my peers is one of them.

Happy Warriors search for the truth.

<u>Chapter 51</u>
The Narrow Gate

"Enter by the narrow gate. For the gate is wide and the way is easy that leads to destruction, and those who enter by it are many. For the gate is narrow and the way is hard that leads to life, and those who find it are few."

Jesus ESV Matthew 7:13-14

VA drugs were part of my life for over 10 years… VA drugs nearly destroyed me

Happy Warriors use the narrow gate.

Chapter 52
No One is Perfect

All have sinned and fall short of the glory of God, being justified as a gift by His grace through the redemption which is in Christ Jesus.

NASB Romans 3:23-24

Perfectionism and happiness go together like cold water and a sleeping bag. Don't get me wrong, at times perfection is very important to me, but...

Happy Warriors give grace to themselves and others.

Chapter 53
Rear View Mirror

Forget the former things; do not dwell on the past. See, I am doing a new thing*!*
NIV Isaiah 43:18-19

Forgetting what lies behind and straining forward to what lies ahead, I press on toward the goal for the prize of the upward call of God in Christ Jesus. Let those of us who are mature think this way, and if in anything you think otherwise, God will reveal that also to you.
ESV Philippians 3:13

My son was in the back seat crying; I had just crashed into the car in front of me. Spending too much time in the rearview mirror eventually causes suffering.
Happy Warriors focus on Jesus.

Chapter 54
Other Gods

You shall have no other gods before me.

ESV Exodus 20:3

My war years were punctuated with brief periods of heavy drinking. This was normal for my shipmates and me. Exotic ports...Hong Kong, Taiwan, the Philippines...all used by the U.S. Navy for rest and relaxation. We would get wild and crazy pretending that Vietnam did not exist. My belief system was falling apart. No amount of alcohol made me happy. But I kept trying more and more alcohol, more and more pretending. No amount of chemicals made me happy. I was searching for happiness in all the wrong places. One definition of insanity is doing the same thing over and over again expecting different results.

Happy Warriors search for the Truth.

Chapter 55

Pride is a Thief

God opposes the proud but gives grace to the humble.

ESV James 4:6

"Whoever then humbles himself as this child, he is the greatest in the kingdom of heaven."

Jesus NASB Matthew 18:4

My best friend was building a new house. Having a little free time, I went over to help. The site had been prepared for the concrete foundation. We were carrying plywood from the pickup truck to the site. Thick sheets of plywood, heavy plywood. In those days I was a weightlifter and decided to show off for my buddy, and instead of the appropriate one sheet at a time, I thought it would be a good idea to carry two at the same time by myself.

Everything was going well until I got to a small downslope. My foot slipped and I went down with the plywood on top of me twisting my knee and my ankle. My father used to say "Pride goes before a fall." In this case it certainly did. I was humiliated and in pain. My ankle hurt so bad that night I could not sleep.

Happy Warriors are humble.

Chapter 56
Be Thankful

Rejoice always, pray without ceasing, give thanks in all circumstances; for this is the will of God in Christ Jesus for you.

NASB 1 Thessalonians 5:16-18

My time in the mental hospital was both wonderful and horrible. After about a year and a half in the cage I got really sick. I was so sick I realized the hospital would be fine as long as I wasn't sick. After two days of throwing up and sitting on the toilet I was thankful to be well, even if I was in a cage.

Happy Warriors are thankful.

Chapter 57
Trials

Count it all joy, my brothers, when you meet trials of various kinds, for you know that the testing of your faith produces steadfastness. And let steadfastness have its full effect, that you may be perfect and complete, lacking in nothing.

ESV James 1:2-4

The United States Navy knows how to get young people into shape for war. Sea trials are an important part of Navy life. At times we hated the training, difficult and repetitive, but somewhere deep inside we all knew that it was very important.

Happy Warriors value training.

Chapter 58

Gasoline on the Fire

Wine is a mocker and beer a brawler.

NIV Proverbs 20:1

One of my favorite roommates at the mental hospital was an Iraq War veteran. My friend and I shared many stories. We both used humor to deal with our dreadful situation... the cage. After many months together, I felt comfortable enough to ask him if he ever drank. He replied, "gasoline on the fire."

Happy Warriors are chemical cautious.

Chapter 59

Respect

"Render to Caesar the things that are Caesar's, and to God the things that are God's."

Jesus ESV Matthew 22:21

"Treat others the same way you want them to treat you."

Jesus NASB Luke 6:31

The military salute originated with warriors that were wearing armor. The right hand went up to open their visor when passing another armored warrior. This acknowledged the other warrior had been seen. It is a way of showing that you see and respect the other person and are not afraid of them.

Happy Warriors show respect.

<u>Chapter 60</u>
Failure

We wanted to come to you—I, Paul, again and again—but Satan hindered us.
ESV 1 Thessalonians 2:18

Kudos to the state of Oregon for getting me off the psych meds. Titration off all the VA psychotropic drugs took six months. To say that this was a difficult time for me would be an understatement. Inappropriate psychotropic drug therapy had nearly cost me my life. The hope of freedom kept me going during the titration process; you see, in the beginning I thought I would get to go home after I was off all the psych meds. I had assumed that the powers that be understood that my insanity was completely the result of inappropriate drug therapy. I was terribly wrong. To top it all off, the Oregon State

Hospital was charging me for my lovely stay. Each and every month they would hand me a bill with an updated balance. The Oregon State Hospital was charging me approximately $23,000 dollars each and every month. The time of my release hearing was fast approaching. I was so excited! I thought I was going to get to go home and get my life back to normal. An interesting word, "normal." My peers helped me to understand that normal is just a setting for the washing machine. The big day arrived, and I was ready to go home. Neatly shaved, hair brushed back, and wearing my Sunday best! What a great day this is going to be, I thought to myself, I'll go home and celebrate with a few beers, My family will be so happy.

"Mr. Branch you are appropriately placed here at the Oregon State Hospital… You have the right to an appeal… you have the right to another hearing in six months." said the voice I will never forget. I was devastated, and I couldn't believe I wasn't going home. There were forces beyond my understanding working against me. I had done everything perfectly. Model patient, great self-control without psychotropic drugs. I was devastated.

Happy Warriors know that life is not fair.

Chapter 61
Life is Difficult

"Come to Me, all who are weary and heavy-laden, and I will give you rest. Take My yoke upon you and learn from Me, for I am gentle and humble in heart, and you will find rest for your souls. For My yoke is easy and My burden is light."

Jesus NASB Matthew 11:28-30

The Oregon Cascade mountains are both rugged and beautiful. Teeming with wildlife, the high lakes are filled with fish. I hope I never forget the summer my father, uncle, grandfather and I went on a long back packing trip. We all slept side-by-side under a makeshift lean to. Not yet a teenager, I was so excited to be with the men doing manly things - building a shelter, campfires at night and actually during the day too (so that we could cook), using crawdad tails for bait to catch our food. Wonderful indeed for a young man. I was not strong enough for the hike in. Doing the best I could to be manly, I just wasn't strong enough. Just when I thought I could go no further, I felt my backpack lighten. I did not understand what was going on until I saw my dad behind me. One hand lifting the bottom of my backpack. He was a huge man and very strong. His backpack was filled with beer and canned food. What a wonderful time.

Happy Warriors team up well.

<u>Chapter 62</u>
Security

"I told you, and you do not believe; the works that I do in My Father's name, these testify of Me. But you do not believe because you are not of My sheep. My sheep hear My voice, and I know them, and they follow me, and I give eternal life to them, and they will never perish; and no one will snatch them out of my hand. My Father, who has given them to me, is greater than all; and no one is able to snatch them out of the Father's hand. I and the father are one."

Jesus NASB John 10:25-30

Petty Officer Third Class. I was so glad to make rank. No longer would I have to stand mess duty. Although I did like my high-tech potato peeler. My potato peeler looked like a washing machine with very rough walls. Spraying the potatoes with water while on spin cycle, the walls would rub the peelings off. I forgot about my potatoes only once because when I came back, they were all worn down to tiny little chips. Wasting food is a no-no in the military. Also, I was getting a pay raise! To my surprise my Chief told me I was going to have to stand shore patrol duty for three months. I did not want to, but I had to. I had a driver's license for Japan, so they had me driving a lock up van down at the Honcho; that was the bar district located directly outside the main gate of the Yokosuka naval base. I would arrest drunks. Occasionally I would guard the base at night. I slept well at night knowing somebody else was watching my back.

Happy Warriors feel secure.

Chapter 63

Shut up! Shut up!

He himself bore our sins in His body on the cross, so that we might die to sin and live to righteousness; for by his wounds you were healed.

NASB 1 Peter 2:24

By grace you have been saved through faith; and that not of yourselves, it is the gift of God; not as a result of works, so that no one may boast.

NASB Ephesians 2:8-9

An explosion of sound behind me caused my heart to race. Jumping forward and turning to defend myself, I looked down to see one of my peers in a pitiful state. He was kneeling on the floor screaming. Hands covering his ears, eyes tightly closed and his head bowed, screaming "shut up! shut up! shut up!"

Voices - relentless voices tormenting my peers. A few days after a violent attack on a fellow patient I asked my peer… why? He solemnly responded, "If I don't do what my voices tell me to do, they punish me."

My beliefs try to manipulate me, but rarely succeed. I have learned how to respond to the negative beliefs… Jesus died for that sin also.

Happy Warriors know what Jesus did for them.

Chapter 64
Self-Confidence

For we are the circumcision; who worship by the Spirit of God and glory in Christ Jesus and put no confidence in the flesh.

ESV Philippians 3:3

I can do all things through him who strengthens me.

NASB Philippians 4:13

Migraine headaches and smoke detectors can be very useful, but action must be taken.

John O. Branch Chimney Sweep had grown to be one of the most successful businesses of its kind in the United States. I was self-confident. Opening a fireplace shop seemed like the right thing to do, but lack of capital and retail experience soon put me into a high-pressure situation

Trans ischemic attacks and blinding migraine headaches, the result of my self-confidence.

Always pushing myself, telling myself to just try harder, just work harder. I can do this. I can make this happen. I can force this to happen out of sheer willpower. I can make this happen. Again and again I would tell myself these things. In my late 40s as my body was beginning to shut down. Baffled by my strokes and migraines, doctors gave me pills. Occasionally, my father would say "pride goes before a fall." I think he was trying to tell me something.

Happy Warriors ask for help.

Chapter 65
Death

"I am the resurrection and the life; he who believes in Me will live even if he dies, and everyone who lives and believes in Me will never die."

Jesus NASB John 11:25-26

Death is a nasty thing. When I was in my 30s, my grandmother was diagnosed with cancer. Terminal cancer. My grandmother had been very good to me, and I loved her very much. I knew my grandparents were going to die, but she was only in her mid-70s I thought she should live a lot longer. Hours before her death I went to visit her. This was horribly difficult for me, and of course it was difficult for her–she was dying, not me. I was very nervous. I had high anxiety. Anyway, this made everything horrible. She was in terrible pain. It was all she could do to talk and then she asked me the question, a one-word question, and I knew what she meant. My grandmother asked me "why?" I said, I don't know grandma, but I'll see you in heaven. She passed away shortly after that. Crying was rare in those days, my emotions were so screwed up.

Happy Warriors look forward to going home.

<u>Chapter 66</u>
Grace

By grace you have been saved through faith; and that not of yourselves, it is the gift of God; not as a result of works, so that no one may boast.

NASB Ephesians 2:8-9

When I was 17 years old, and new to the Navy, one of my duty stations was the USS Providence CLG 6. We did lots of training on the Providence. If it doesn't move, paint it or clean it. Seemed to me all we ever did was paint, clean, and train for war. I actually had a lot of fun. I was young and naïve but I enjoyed myself hanging out with the older sailors. Occasionally some of my shipmates and I would drink beer at the base club. Obviously they weren't checking ID there. One night, while trying to fit in, I drank too much.

Being seventeen, and not used to alcohol, this was easy to do. I decided to leave the club early and walked back to the ship alone. The cool night air felt nice but my thoughts went negative. I began to think about the Navy lying to me. They lied to me about being a helicopter mechanic. This was so wrong, they lied to me, how can they do that? The beer made things worse; I got angry. The beer made rational thought impossible.

I climbed the mast. Young and dumb I thought it would be a good idea to spit on the Marines that were guarding the quarter deck. Angry and drunk I decided to do something very stupid and dangerous. Climbing the mast, I worked my way out over the Quarterdeck on the starboard side. Then I started to spit on the Marines that were standing guard. These were well armed Marines. Little time went by before they figured out that they were being spat upon. Like a squirrel I scurried down the mast. My bunk felt extra special that night.

I had outsmarted the Marines. Being young and dumb I thought it would be a good idea to boast about my hijinks to a few of my shipmates. What I had done was extremely dangerous. If the radar had been turned on, I could've been killed. One of my shipmates realized this and ratted me out.

Officers country is "no man's land" for enlisted crew members. So I was very nervous the day my division officer summoned me to his quarters. He asked me if I had climbed the mast and spit on the Marines. Of course I did what any 17-year-old boy would do… I lied.

The interrogation went on for a bit then he changed course and began a very long lecture. I held fast to my lie. My punishment could have been severe, but my superior decided to have mercy on me, and he let me go.

Happy Warriors give grace to themselves and others.

Chapter 67
Self-Loathing

"You shall love your neighbor as yourself."

Jesus ESV Matthew 22:39

I am of the flesh, sold under sin. For I do not understand my own actions. For I do not do what I want, but I do the very thing I hate.

ESV Romans 7:14-15

The fruit of the spirit is love, joy, peace, patience, kindness, goodness, faithfulness, gentleness, self-control; against such things there is no law.

NASB Galatians 5:22-23

Life and death situations in Vietnam were the stimulus for my perfectionism. I knew that I had to do my job perfectly or my shipmates could die. After Vietnam I stowed my perfectionism in my sea-bag along with the rest of my gear. Civilian life has been more difficult than war to understand, my voices always standing by to remind me of my imperfections. My shipmates and I fought many battles together. We were highly aware of the danger, but our love for each other made us strong.

Feeling alone, civilian life was confusing... my shipmates were gone, and I did not know who the enemy was. My beliefs were always ready to remind me of my imperfections. Some of my beliefs were telling me that I was defective and blaming me for terrible things over which I actually had no control. My shipmates and I cheered with joy the night that one of our rounds made a direct hit on an enemy torpedo boat. One round of Willie Peter had been mistakenly loaded, burning alive our enemy. They were trying to kill us, and we were delighted that we were able to neutralize that threat, but my voices continued to tell me how wrong it was. My beliefs were always ready to shame me… even if it was a sin… Jesus died for that sin too!

Happy Warriors love themselves.

<u>Chapter 68</u>
Rules

"Render to Caesar the things that are Caesar's, and to God the things that are God's."

Jesus ESV Matthew 22:21

One of my prescribers suggested that I keep taking benzodiazepines; "Mr. Branch, I highly recommend that you stay at the dose you're on now. You are in a very high stress environment." Every two weeks these words tempted me, but I was determined to be drug free. During the six-month titration process I read many books, including the Bible. Titration off of benzos was one of the hardest things I've ever done. I'm now very thankful for my time in the cage. After an especially difficult day, I decided to take a shower to relax. Soon these words started coming out of my mouth over and over again, I said, "they are just the rules, they don't have to make sense. An epiphany that's what this is… an Epiphany." I felt confusion and burden lifted from me. *They are just the rules, they don't have to make sense!* For a very long time I had been trying to make sense of my new social system. Loony bin, nuthouse. My peers and I would empower ourselves with slang that was forbidden. Oregon State Hospital or Hospital were the acceptable. They are just the rules, they don't have to make sense. I felt something new…peace. Wow. I now have something new to share with my peers. When I climbed into the shower, I had no idea today was going to be special. I was drying my hair with a towel when I realized the treasure I had discovered. *They are just the rules, they don't have to make sense.* Social structures… all of them designed and remodeled by humans. Humans are imperfect; anything humans design and build is going to be imperfect. I need to remember this. I am imperfect, my creations will be imperfect. I need to give myself and others grace. Jesus is perfect… We are not. This truly is a good day… thank you!

Happy Warriors follow the rules.

<u>Chapter 69</u>
Focus

Therefore, since we have so great a cloud of witnesses surrounding us, let us also lay aside every encumbrance and the sin which so easily entangles us, and let us run with endurance the race that is set before us, fixing our eyes on Jesus, the author and perfecter of faith, who for the joy set before him endured the cross, despising the shame and has sat down at the right-hand of the throne of God.

NASB Hebrews 12:1-2

My dad and I were deer hunting in Central Oregon when at least a dozen deer walked in front of us. We opened fire. The deer immediately scattered frantically... we kept shooting. Not one deer was injured. It was amazing that we could miss when they were so close. We did not hit our target because we did not select a specific target. Later that day a young buck came running by at full speed. My 1950s era 30 30 Winchester rifle went to my shoulder. Taking aim with the open sites, a gentle squeeze of the trigger was all it took to send this little buck to deer Heaven.

Happy Warriors focus.

Chapter 70

Be Still

Be still, and know that I am God.

ESV Psalm 46:10

In the 1950s and early 60s there was a television show that featured talented people from all over the globe. Singers and dancers, acrobats—you name it—talented people showing off their skills. My family and I watched the Ed Sullivan show every Sunday night. When we saw the Beatles perform live, I remember mom and dad talking about how long the performers' hair was. Another act on the show that stands out in my mind was a man who would spin dinner plates on poles. Running back and forth keeping the momentum going on the plates, he would add more poles and more plates. Of course, if he added enough poles and plates, he would not be able to keep the momentum going and the plates would start falling. I still have a tendency to do that in my life... keep adding more and more until the plates start falling... I think I need to learn something.

Happy Warriors don't try to do everything themselves.

Chapter 71
Yeah... And

Christ also died for sins once for all, the just for the unjust, so that he might bring us to God, having been put to death in the flesh, but made alive in the spirit.

NASB 1 Peter 3:18

If we confess our sins, he is faithful and just to forgive us our sins and to cleanse us from all unrighteousness.

ESV 1 John 1:9

The Oregon State Hospital was a wonderful-horrible experience for me. I learned so much from my peers, so many kind and wonderful people tormented by voices. People covering their ears and screaming "Shut up" to their unseen tormentors. People behaving badly because their voices had told them to do it, or else. My peers had given their voices power. My peers live in fear of their voices, turning over self-control to the unseen tyrants. The voices that remind me of my past sins are not my friends. The sword of the Spirit cuts through all the lies… Jesus died for that sin too.

Happy Warriors respond appropriately to all voices.

Chapter 72
East from West

The Lord is compassionate and gracious, slow to anger and abounding in loving kindness. He will not always strive with us, nor will he keep his anger forever. He has not dealt with us according to our sins, nor rewarded us according to our iniquities. For as high as the heavens are above the earth, so great is his loving kindness toward those who fear him. As far as the east is from the west, so far has he removed our transgressions from us. Just as a father has compassion on his children, so the lord has compassion on those who fear him. For He himself knows our frame; He is mindful that we are but dust.

NASB Psalm 103:8-14

My teenage years were a nightmare for my parents. At age 16 I told my parents I wanted to join the Navy. My father immediately told me I was an idiot, which may have been true but not helpful communication. Eleven days after my 17th birthday I left home for San Diego, California.

My father enjoyed tormenting me occasionally with my history.

The voice I listen to never reminds me of my past sins.

Happy Warriors listen to the one who loves them.

Chapter 73
The Chaplain

Do not neglect to show hospitality to strangers, for by this some have entertained angels without knowing it.

NASB Hebrews 13:1-2

Devastated by the results of the hearing, depression was starting to set in. Then I heard a voice barking commands: *stand up straight, keep shaving, keep going to treatment mall.*

I had been walking down the hall with my head slumped to the ground; even without drugs I was beginning to do the Thorazine shuffle. How can they do this to me? I've done everything perfectly; I don't understand. Why me?

Following my new orders, I stood up straight, went back to my room, and shaved.

Later, the same voice told me he was a Chaplin. He asked me if I would like to pray with him, I have never heard anybody pray like that—he sounded terrified! Then he was gone.

I don't remember ever experiencing anything so strange.

Happy Warriors are careful with assumptions.

Chapter 74
WAR

Dear friends, I urge you, as foreigners and exiles, to abstain from sinful desires, which wage war against your soul.

NIV 1 Peter 2:11

The USS Providence CLG had a brig. An actual jail. It was located near our berthing compartment. When someone got in trouble he would be locked in the cage. Marines would guard him, Unpleasant to say the least.

Three days bread and water for one wayward sailor. Seemed very strange to me… in the cage with a loaf of bread and water… strange punishment. He probably lost rank also, maybe the loss of liberty and pay for a while. My point is, this got my attention. I did not want to be put in that cage.

Happy Warriors control themselves.

<u>Chapter 75</u>
Shame

Jesus, the author and perfecter of faith, who for the joy set before Him endured the cross, despising the shame, and has sat down at the right-hand of the throne of God.

NASB Hebrews 12:2

For I am not ashamed of the gospel, for it is the power of God for salvation to everyone who believes.

ESV Romans 1:16

One of my treatment mall classes was "Shame Resilience," taught by two doctors of psychology. I'm sure both doctors meant well, but the group did nothing but further shame all of us. You see, all of us were men except the lead facilitator.

The course book was written by a woman for women. I was the only one in the group to read the entire book, (I was doing everything I could to earn my freedom). We were almost through with the book when one of my peers finally realized, "This book is for women." He blurted it out.

Happy Warriors point to Jesus when shamed.

Chapter 76
Born Again

"That which is born of the flesh is flesh, and that which is born of the spirit is spirit. Do not be amazed that I said to you, you must be born again. The wind blows where it wishes and you hear the sound of it, but do not know where it comes from and where it is going; so is everyone who is born of the Spirit."

Jesus NASB John 3:6-8

Radar and sonar are essential to function on a modern warship, allowing us to see what is important.

Happy Warriors train their senses.

Chapter 77
One Bite at a Time

"Do not worry about tomorrow; for tomorrow will care for itself. Each day has enough trouble of its own."

Jesus NASB Matthew 6:34

Business was good. My employees were happy, and I was expanding my business into a retail store. Always looking to the future, always looking to make more money, never able to enjoy what I had. Constantly searching for that next mission. Blinding migraine headaches and strokes got my attention. Life is like eating a brontosaurus... take small bites.

Happy Warriors are content.

<u>Chapter 78</u>
John Wayne

"If you abide in Me, and My words abide in you, ask whatever you wish, and it will be done for you. My Father is glorified by this, that you bear much fruit, and so prove to be My disciples."

Jesus NASB John 15:7-8

My best friend was tired. It was late and now dark, but he wanted more firewood. Taking a mighty swing with a heavy splitting mall, the clothesline pulled the Ax into his forehead... I could see his brain. My prayer was short and intense... please don't let Marty die, and please take away all the pain. After a night filled with surgery, Marty said he did not need any pain medication. The nurse sarcastically replied we do not need any

John Waynes here today. Marty replied, "I have no pain."

Happy Warriors ask for help.

Chapter 79
Actions Speak Louderthan Words

Show me your faith apart from your works, and I will show you my faith by my works. You believe that God is one; you do well. Even the demons believe—and shudder! Do you want to be shown, you foolish person, that faith apart from works is useless?

ESV James 2:18-20

Do you know how to tell when a politician is lying? Their lips are moving. During the late 70s I worked as a real estate salesman. If you want to make money in real estate you have to really hustle. I was working very hard, college classes, seminars, any and all trainings that I could attend I would; this was my new career. A high school friend of mine called me...

I thought he was just checking up to see how I was. Then he started asking me questions about the local real estate market. I helped him quite a bit. After several days he said to me, "John, I'm not trying to use you." I had not given thought to the possibility of him using me, Only then did I realize that he was actually using me; He had no intention of buying property through me. This was only one of many experiences that helped me to understand that actions speak louder than words.

Happy Warriors act on truth.

Chapter 80
Wealth

The brother of humble circumstances is to glory in his high position; and the rich man is to glory in his humiliation.

NASB James 1:9-10

"How difficult it will be for those who have wealth to enter the kingdom of God!"

Jesus ESV Mark 10:23

Payday came twice a month in the navy, and they paid us in cash. We did not make very much money, usually just enough to have fun with. I would keep my cash in a little square can in my foot locker. Very little money, but I had purpose which gave me true wealth, I was happy.

My years in real estate sales were confusing. Some of my associates were very wealthy. Money was my new focus. I was having scotch for lunch. Very confusing. My wife left me, and my anxiety was out-of-control. Pain and confusion filled my days and nights. My belief system was a mess. I was looking for happy in all the wrong places.

I hated Vietnam, but I had purpose there. My shipmates were my purpose; we kept each other alive. This time was so intense. Always in the back of my mind was fear. Intense fear of being a prisoner of war. Vietnam gave me purpose, war gave me my shipmates, life made sense. Civilian life is confusing; I did not understand the rules.

Happy Warriors are wealthy.

<u>Chapter 81</u>
Sarcasm

"If anyone is thirsty, let him come to Me and drink. He who believes in Me, as the Scripture said, from his innermost being will flow rivers of living water."

Jesus NASB John 7:37-38

My little sister and my best friend have both shared with me the fact that sarcasm is always aggression.

Happy Warriors are skilled in the use of all weapons.

Chapter 82
Slavery

We also once were foolish ourselves, disobedient, deceived, enslaved to various lusts and pleasures, spending our life in malice and envy, hateful, hating one another. But when the kindness of God our Savior and His love for mankind appeared, He saved us, not on the basis of deeds which we have done in righteousness, but according to his mercy, by the washing of regeneration and renewing by the Holy Spirit, whom he poured out upon us richly through Jesus Christ our Savior, so that being justified by his grace we would be made heirs according to the hope of eternal life.

NASB Titus 3:3-7

Grace... that's the reason I'm alive today. War, fast motorcycles, wild partying… so many reasons I should be dead right now.

Happy Warriors are not foolish.

<u>Chapter 83</u>
Mission

See that you fulfill the ministry that you have received in the Lord.

ESV Colossians 4:17

Building yourselves up in your most holy faith and praying in the Holy Spirit keep yourselves in the love of God, waiting for the mercy of our Lord Jesus Christ that leads to eternal life. And have mercy on those who doubt; save others by snatching them out of the fire; to others show mercy with fear, hating even the garment stained by the flesh.

ESV Jude:20-23

The USS Rowan DD 782 was equipped with nuclear capable anti-submarine rockets. ASROC. I carried a Navy issue Colt 45 caliber sidearm. We stood watch 24 7. We knew that our enemies were powerful and always working hard to destroy us. We knew our mission.

Happy Warriors know their mission.

Chapter 84

Their Agenda

Perceiving then that they were about to come and take him by force to make him king, Jesus withdrew again to the mountain by himself.

ESV John 6:15

My tendency is to be like the man on the Ed Sullivan show, adding spinning plates until everything comes crashing down around me.

When other people try to draw me into their world of good intentions, I have trouble saying no.

Occasionally I remember the wisdom of my employee…"bloody hell John, you're not Superman."

Happy Warriors have their own agenda.

<u>Chapter 85</u>

Normal

Then he went home, and the crowd gathered again, so that they could not even eat. And when his family heard it, they went out to seize him, for they were saying, "He is out of his mind."

ESV Mark 3:20-21

Normal is just a setting for washing machines... this is what I learned at the Oregon State Hospital.

Happy Warriors are unique.

Chapter 86
Good People

"No one is good except God alone."
Jesus NASB Mark 10:18

Doing time at the Oregon State Hospital is difficult. As patients progress, they are sometimes allowed to go on outings. A chance to ride in a van and maybe grab some fast food is something that gives hope. Carrot on a stick sort of thing.

Two staff members and a half dozen of my peers were in the van. It was a real privilege to be able to leave the hospital for a couple of hours. My peers and I looked forward to this once a week trip. If we follow all the rules we would get to go on our outing—our reward for being good. As I was putting my seatbelt on, I realized I'd forgotten my ID card. We were not allowed to go anywhere without our hospital ID card. How could I have forgotten this? Thoughts… *don't say anything maybe no one will notice and I can get away with this*. I quickly decided that the risk and the punishment would be too great, so I confessed my mistake to the staff. Everybody was groaning. I was being shamed for my mistake. This would eat up part of our time. One of the staffers would have to take me back to my room, this was humiliating, I had made a mistake. If I was good, I would be good all the time. If my peers were good, they would be good all the time. As we walked back to my room to retrieve my ID card I said to the staffer "This proves it." "Proves what?" I replied, "I am not perfect." Immediately I felt the pressure go away.

Happy Warriors understand no one is perfect.

Chapter 87
I Can Do This

I can do all things through Christ who strengthens me.

NKJV Philippians 4:13

Business was good! I was making plenty of money and I was happy. Every morning before work I would say a little prayer "Heavenly Father please help me to do perfect work today, and please cause all my customers to know that I'm doing the best job possible for them." I was not focused on money, I was happy. I was focused on doing the best job possible for my customers; I was not focused on myself. I was focused on my customers and I knew I was not perfect, so I asked for help. Happy Warriors ask for help.

Chapter 88
Goals

Come now, you who say, "Today or tomorrow we will go into such and such a town and spend a year there and trade and make a profit"—yet you do not know what tomorrow will bring. What is your life? For you are a mist that appears for a little time and then vanishes. Instead you ought to say, "If the Lord wills, we will live and do this or that." As it is, you boast in your arrogance. All such boasting is evil.
ESV James 4:13-16

One of my goals as a young man was to be a helicopter mechanic. When I signed my enlistment papers my recruiter promised me that I would be a helicopter mechanic. My recruiter's promise was not kept, I felt betrayed, and for many years, decades, I held onto my bitterness. The

Navy changed my plans leading to different life experiences. All of my experiences have led me to where I am today... happy!

Happy Warriors are flexible.

Chapter 89

Worry

The Lord is my shepherd, I shall not want. He makes me lie down in green pastures; he leads me beside quiet waters. He restores my soul; he guides me in the paths of righteousness for His name's sake. Even though I walk through the valley of the shadow of death, I fear no evil, for you are with me; your rod and your staff, they comfort me. You prepare a table before me in the presence of my enemies; you have anointed my head with oil; my cup overflows. Surely goodness and lovingkindness will follow me all the days of my life, and I will dwell in the house of the lord forever.

NASB Psalm 23

Every day had one thing in common in Vietnam… I trusted my commanding officer.

During typhoons my captain would stay awake on the bridge to make sure we all survived. He earned my respect for this. I was actually able to enjoy storms because there was no Chow-line. Combat was terrifying, but I always knew our captain would get us through it.

Happy Warriors trust their commanding officer.

<u>Chapter 90</u>
My Compass

God willed to make known what is the riches of the glory of this mystery among the Gentiles, which is Christ in you, the hope of glory.

NASB Colossians 1:27

The fruit of the Spirit is love, Joy, peace, patience, kindness, goodness, faithfulness, gentleness, self-control.

NASB Galatians 5:22-23

Portland VA hospital doctors diagnosed me with PTSD. The course of action they chose was to fill me with chemicals. VA prescription drugs were added, and dose levels modified until the VA drove me completely insane. I did not have a chemical imbalance until I went to the Portland VA Hospital. The VA prescribed me drugs. Inappropriate VA drug therapy cost me dearly, nearly cost me my life. I had 22 years of freedom from tobacco, then VA drug therapy drove me to begin chain-smoking. I had a faulty belief system, not a chemical imbalance. I know I am off course when I'm not experiencing love, joy, peace, patience, kindness, goodness, faithfulness, gentleness and self-control… I now trust my compass!

Happy Warriors have excellent self-control.

<u>Chapter 91</u>

Honor

"If anyone serves me, he must follow me; and where I am, there will my servant be also. If anyone serves me, the father will honor him."

Jesus, ESV John 12:26

"I do not seek my own glory; there is One who seeks it, and he is the judge"

Jesus ESV John 8:50

My war medals were awarded to me. I did not ask for them. Someone higher than me determined I was worthy of the praise.

Happy Warriors do not glorify themselves.

Chapter 92
Power

"I lay down my life so that I may take it up again. No one has taken it away from Me, but I lay it down on My own initiative, I have authority to lay it down, and I have authority to take it up again. This commandment I received from my father."

Jesus NASB John 10:17-18

I recently saw a video of a wounded veteran receiving the Congressional Medal of Honor. I am still moved to tears when I think about what he had done to earn the medal. He had thrown himself on top of a live grenade. Everybody survived because this veteran's body absorbed the full punishment that was meant for his friends. Incredible!

Happy Warriors are powerful.

Chapter 93
They Laughed at Me

They laughed at him. But he put them all outside and took the child's father and mother and those who were with him and went in where the child was.

ESV Mark 4:40

Titration behind me, I realized I needed to start trusting my own judgment.

Happy Warriors ignore the critics.

<u>Chapter 94</u>

Love the Truth

With all wicked deception for those who are perishing, because they refused to love the truth and so be saved.

ESV 2 Thessalonians 2:10

One of my peers at the Oregon State Hospital was drug-free... no psych meds. This is very rare. I believe there were only three of us. On occasion, my friend would wear a T-shirt that said "Truth." Being drug-free, he could see things that other people could not. My friend was incarcerated for up to five years. Oregon State law at the time was quite clear: patients must be released if they are no longer a danger to themselves or others or they are no longer mentally ill. My peer shared with me his frustration with the powers that be. He was convinced that he was being punished for offending someone in power. He was not released until every day of the five years was spent in the hospital.

Happy Warriors love the truth.

<u>Chapter 95</u>
Be Nice

"If you then, who are evil, know how to give good gifts to your children, how much more will your Father who is in heaven give good things to those who ask him! So whatever you wish that others would do to you, do also to them, for this is the law and the prophets."

Jesus ESV Matthew 7:11-12

Doctors at the Oregon State Hospital described me as a model patient. As much as possible, I treated my peers and staff the way I wanted to be treated.

Happy Warriors control themselves.

Chapter 96
Cancer

"It is not those who are healthy who need a physician, but those who are sick. But go and learn what this means: I desire compassion, and not sacrifice, for I did not come to call the righteous, but sinners."

Jesus Matthew 9:12-13

"I don't understand this Mr. Branch, your cancer is gone."

"Hallelujah thank you Jesus!" Confused and now startled by my shouts of joy, my surgeon said, "I don't know what happened your cancer is gone." Dramatic answer to my prayers had filled me with joy, and my surgeon with confusion.

Happy Warriors never give up.

<u>Chapter 97</u>
Truth

"God is Spirit, and those who worship him must worship in spirit and truth."

Jesus ESV John 4:24

"I am the way, and the truth, and the life; no one comes to the Father but through me."

Jesus NASB John 14:6

"You Will know the truth, and the truth will make you free."

Jesus NASB John 8:32

I thoroughly enjoyed my time as a real estate appraiser. Banks and mortgage companies would hire me to tell them the truth. What is the true value of this property? I would go to the property, take photographs, measure the inside and out-side of the improvements, explore the immediate surroundings, and take photographs of comparable properties. Then I would go back to my office, and examine government records. Compiling all the data I would examine the facts, and weigh the evidence. Finally, I would prepare my report and personally hand it to my client. Before making their decision to loan substantial amounts of money, they wanted to know the truth.

Happy Warriors value the truth.

Chapter 98
The Tongue

No one can tame the tongue; it is a restless evil and full of deadly poison.

NASB James 3:8

Does a fountain send out from the same opening both fresh and bitter water?

NASB James 3:11

"Blithering idiot" were the last words out of my mouth before I hit the ground, stunned by the powerful slap. My father may have earned the insult but it was my tongue that was causing my pain.

Happy Warriors are word-cautious.

<u>Chapter 99</u>
The Gift

By grace you have been saved through faith. And this is not your own doing; it is the gift of God, not a result of works, so that no one may boast.

ESV Ephesians 2:8-9

My grandfather gave me a Honda 50 when I was 12. This was a wonderful gift. I loved that motorcycle. It was the best gift that I had ever received. Every day after school and on weekends, I was out in the cow pasture enjoying my gift. I had done nothing to earn this gift, but there I was, my hair blowing in the wind and a smile on my face.

Happy Warriors take nothing for granted.

<u>Chapter 100</u>

Grenades

Then Simon Peter, having a sword, drew it and struck the high priest's servant and cut off his right ear. So Jesus said to Peter, "Put your sword into its sheath; shall I not drink the cup that the father has given me?"

ESV John 18:10-11

Weapons division aboard the USS Rowan was a perfect fit for me. Every day and everything was exciting and dangerous. We had an armory filled with powerful weapons... very dangerous and powerful weapons.

One day, the morning sun was warming my back, and the fresh sea air was caressing my face when one of our gunner's mates handed me something I'd never seen before. It was about the size and shape of a large hairspray can, only much heavier. Like a slap in the face, I noticed the pin, "this thing is a grenade!" I blurted.

The old salt began to give me the rundown on how our enemies would sometimes try to sneak up on us underwater. I knew this would be impossible without a submarine because we were steaming through the water at at least 10 knots. My shipmate informed me that if for some reason we went dead in the water our enemies could swim underwater and plant explosives on our hull. With a twinkle in his eye he said "pull the pin and drop one of the these over the side, and our problem goes to meet his ancestors!"

Happy Warriors are weapons-cautious.

Chapter 101
Contentment

I have learned to be content in whatever circumstances I am. I know how to get along with humble means, and I also know how to live in prosperity; in any and every circumstance I have learned the secret of being filled and going hungry, both of having abundance and suffering need. I can do all things through him who strengthens me.

NASB Philippians 4:11-13

A very long time ago my father shared some wisdom with me. "John, the happiest time in a man's life is when he is carrying a lunchbox to work." These words ring true for me now that I've missed out on so much by not being content.

Happy Warriors are content.

<u>Chapter 102</u>
Promises

And the king said to the girl, "Ask me for whatever you wish, and I will give it to you." And he vowed to her, "Whatever you ask me, I will give you, up to half my kingdom." And she went out and said to her mother, "For what should I ask?" And she said, "The head of John the Baptist." And she came in immediately with haste to the king and asked, saying, "I want you to give me at once the head of John the Baptist on a platter." And the king was exceedingly sorry, but because of his oaths and his guests he did not want to break his word to her.

ESV Mark 6:22-26

My promises have caused some no-win situations in my life. My broken promises have caused a great deal of suffering.

Happy Warriors are promise—careful.

Chapter 103
Glory

"How can you believe, when you receive glory from one another and do not seek the glory that comes from the only God?"

Jesus ESV John 5:44

Off the coast of Vietnam, we received a radio call for help. Marines asked us to put some rounds on the enemy. We were happy to assist our brothers. Real-life and practice shooting was paying dividends; we destroyed the targets as requested.

Blue sky with white billowy clouds that day. I could hear the sound of the Marine Corps fighter jet before I could see it. Pushing my head out of the hatch of the gun fire control director I was able to see something I'd never seen before: A jet fighter plane flying just above the surface of the ocean and very close to us. Approaching from behind with amazing speed and skill, the pilot roared past us at bridge level. Doing barrel rolls just above the water, the plane pulled straight up. Continuing the barrel rolls, He went out of sight. The guy was good—I mean really good. I felt really excited and happy to receive praise for a job well done.

Happy Warriors value glory.

Chapter 104
The Race

Lay aside every encumbrance and the sin which so easily entangles us, and let us run with endurance the race that is set before us, fixing our eyes on Jesus, the author and perfecter of faith, who for the joy set before him endured the cross, despising the shame, and has sat down at the right hand of the throne of God.

NASB Hebrews 12:1-2

The Oregon State Hospitalthoroughly tested me; literally and figuratively. Video cameras just about everywhere, chart noting every hour, day, and night, 24-7. And of course, every psychological test known. Well at least that's the way it felt to me. "If you come to the hospital with no mental illness… you will leave with PTSD." I couldn't believe my group facilitator had said this out loud! Realizing his mistake, he refused to comment further.

Punishment is not allowed at the Oregon State Hospital. Everything is therapy. Four hours of treatment mall every day eventually feels like punishment to everybody.

Redundant drug and alcohol training became quite annoying for me. After two years I asked one of my doctors if she thought I had addiction tendencies. She quickly replied "No." Then I immediately thought; The rules are just the rules, they don't have to make sense.

My mental hospital days were at times difficult beyond imagination, but my peers made my incarceration worthwhile.

Many years have passed since I was fully discharged from the Oregon State Hospital. Struggling to tell my story effectively and properly, I realized something was getting in my way.

Then it came to me! My story needs 100% of my brain right now. So, I gave up happy hour.

"Two steps past the finish line is where the race ends." Words of wisdom from my best friend.

Happy Warriors compete to win.

Chapter 105
Chemicals

For you were called to freedom, brothers. Only do not use your freedom as an opportunity for the flesh, but through love serve one another. For the whole law is fulfilled in one word "You shall love your neighbor as yourself." But if you bite and devour one another, watch out that you are not consumed by one another. But I say, walk by the Spirit, and you will not gratify the desires of the flesh. For the desires of the flesh are against the spirit, and the desires of the Spirit are against the flesh, for these are opposed to each other, to keep you from doing the things you want to do. But if you are led by the spirit you are not under the law. Now the works of the flesh are evident: sexual immorality, impurity, sensuality, idolatry, sorcery, enmity, strife, jealousy, fits of anger, rivalries, dissensions, divisions, envy, drunkenness, orgies, and things like these. I warn you, as I warned you before, that those who do such things will not inherit the kingdom of God. But the fruit of the Spirit is love, Joy, peace, patience, kindness, goodness, faithfulness, gentle- ness, self-control; against such things there is no law. And those who belong to Christ Jesus have crucified the flesh with its passions and desires. If we live by the Spirit, let us also keep in step with the Spirit. Let us not become conceited, provoking one another, envying one another.

ESV Galatians 5:13-25

Drugs and/or alcohol always play a role in patient incarceration at the Oregon State Hospital. My peers and I enjoyed sharing our stories with each other and   I could find no exception to the drugs and/or alcohol rule. Patients would suddenly stop their medication without their doctors' advice, causing catastrophe. Alcoholics suddenly stopping their drug of choice. Street drugs of course are always problematic.

Chemicals do not cure belief system problems.

Happy Warriors are Chemical-Cautious.

<u>Chapter 106</u>
Do Not Judge

"Do not judge so that you will not be judged. For in the way you judge, you will be judged; and by your standard of measure, it will be measured to you. Why do you look at the speck that is in your brother's eye, but do not notice the log that is in your own eye? Or how can you say to your brother, let me take the speck out of your eye, and behold, the log is in your own eye?

You hypocrite, first take the log out of your own eye, and then you will see clearly to take the speck out of your brother's eye."

Jesus NASB Matthew 7:1-5

In everything, treat people the same way you want them to treat you.

Jesus NASB Matthew 7:12

Many years ago a good friend of mine shared a problem that he was having. He was quite embarrassed. I politely listened but internally I judged him. Sometime after my inappropriate judgment, I found myself in the same trap he had been in. I was now ashamed and embarrassed. How could I be so blind?

Happy Warriors are not always heroes.

Chapter 107
1968

I do not consider that I have made it my own. But one thing I do: forgetting what lies behind and straining forward to what lies ahead, I press on toward the goal for the prize of the upward call of God in Christ Jesus. Let those of us who are mature think this way, and if in anything you think otherwise, God will reveal that also to you.

ESV Philippians 3:13-16

My last roommate at the Oregon State Hospital was quite a challenge. The man was a fellow combat veteran who served in Vietnam during the 1968 Tet Offensive, a terrible and bloody year. My roommate and I shared similar beliefs, but he was a slave to his past. When voices reminded him he would start repeating "1968…

1968… 1968." Often this happened in our veteran group. Once a week we would get together during treatment mall for mutual support and encouragement. I always looked forward to this time but occasionally my peer would start repeating "1968" over and over again. The rest of us knew to move away from him and let security restrain him and put him into a calm down room. I personally don't know how anybody could calm down while helplessly strapped to a bed.

Happy Warriors do not focus on the past.

Chapter 108

Success

"The last shall be first, and the first last."

Jesus NASB Matthew 20:16

"If anyone would be first, he must be last of all and servant of all."

Jesus ESV Mark 9:35

My time in real estate allowed me to rub shoulders with some very wealthy people. For me, spending time with wealthy people was interesting, fun at times, but also very frustrating. Success in real estate was always measured in dollars. This left me feeling hollow.

Happy Warriors are successful.

Chapter 109
Belief Systems

"Everyone who hears these words of mine and acts on them may be compared to a wise man who built his house on the rock. And the rain fell, and the floods came, and the winds blew and slammed against that house; and yet it did not fall for it had been founded on the rock. Everyone who hears these words of mine and does not act on them will be like a foolish man who built his house on the sand. The rain fell and the floods came and the winds blew and slammed against that house; and it fell—and great was its fall."

Jesus NASB Matthew 7:24-27

Belief systems, like germs, are hard to see, sometimes very destructive, sometimes alive, and sometimes dead. Every human being has germs and belief systems. Some of my beliefs were good for me just like some of my germs, but some of my beliefs were toxic. The bullet that tore through my right lung and my liver marked the beginning of an incredible remodeling project.

My belief system at that time was in shambles. I needed something outside of myself–something painful–something horrible–something powerful to help me take the first bite. Belief system change, like eating a brontosaurus, starts with the first bite. I did not need to tear down my house; I just needed to remodel. Some of my beliefs were good, some not so good. Some were killing me and my family. Foundation is crucial in any structure. This adventure thoroughly tested my foundation.

Happy Warriors have the perfect foundation.

<u>Chapter 110</u>
Eternity

"If anyone would come after me, let him deny himself and take up his cross and follow me. For whoever would save his life will lose it, but whoever loses his life for my sake and the gospel's will save it. For what does it profit a man to gain the whole world and forfeit his soul? For what can a man give in return for his soul? For whoever is ashamed of me and of my words in this adulterous and sinful generation, of him will the son of man also be ashamed when he comes in the glory of his father with the holy angels."

Jesus ESV Mark 8:34-38

I thought my enlistment would never end. Feeling betrayed by the Navy and my country, the time for my discharge seemed forever away. I received my honorable discharge and walked into civilian life.

During my time at the mental hospital, my discharge seemed forever in the future, but like everything else, it came to pass. I received my discharge and walked back into freedom. Time is different when I focus on Jesus.

My time here on planet Earth is tiny compared to forever.

Happy Warriors understand that our time here on planet Earth is tiny compared to Eternity.

I Am

"I am the way, and the truth, and the life. No one comes to the Father except through me."

Jesus ESV John 14:6

My life has been filled with many adventures. Two years of war in Vietnam, husband, father, grandfather, businessman, pilot, I am not those jobs, I am not those titles…

I AM A HAPPY

WARRIOR!

Chapter 111
We Need You!

Please stick around and help the rest of us!

We are not perfect!

Yes, Jesus died for that sin too!

Focus On Jesus

Appendix 1

This appendix includes all Bible verses used in the book. Verses are listed below in Biblical order.

Old Testament

- You shall have no other gods before me. ESV Exodus 20:3 Chapter 54
- The Lord is my shepherd, I shall not want. He makes me lie down in green pastures; he leads me beside quiet waters. He restores my soul; he guides me in the paths of righteousness for His name's sake. Even though I walk through the valley of the shadow of death, I fear no evil, for you are with me; your rod and your staff, they comfort me. You prepare a table before me in the presence of my enemies; you have anointed my head with oil; my

cup overflows. Surely goodness and lovingkindness will follow me all the days of my life, and I will dwell in the house of the lord forever. NASB Psalm 23 Chapter 89

- I will instruct you and teach you in the way you should go; I will counsel you with my eye upon you. ESV Psalm 32:8 Chapter 35

- Be still, and know that I am God. ESV Psalm 46:10 Chapter 70

- The Lord is compassionate and gracious, slow to anger and abounding in loving kindness. He will not always strive with us, nor will he keep his anger forever. He has not dealt with us according to our sins, nor rewarded us according to our iniquities. For as high as the heavens are above the earth, so great is his loving kindness toward those who fear him. As far as the east is from the west, so far has he removed our transgressions from us. Just as a father has compassion on his children, so the lord has compassion on those who fear him. For he himself knows our frame; He is mindful that we are but dust. NASB Psalm 103 8-14 Chapter 72

- The fear of the Lord is the beginning of wisdom, and the knowledge of the Holy One is understanding. NASB Proverbs 9:10 Chapter 20

- The mind of the intelligent seeks knowledge, but the mouth of fools feed on folly. NASB Proverbs 15 14 Chapter 24

- Better is a little with the fear of the Lord than great treasure and turmoil with it. NASB Proverbs 15 16 Chapter 24

- Wine is a mocker and beer a brawler. NIV Proverbs 20:1 Chapter 58

- Every man's way is right in his own eyes, but the Lord weighs the hearts. NASB Proverbs 21:2 Chapter 42

- Iron sharpens iron, So one man sharpens another. NASB Proverbs 27:17 Chapter 36

- Forget the former things; do not dwell on the past. See, I am doing a new thing! NIV Isaiah 43:18-19 Chapter 53

New Testament

- "Blessed are those who hunger and thirst for righteousness, for they shall be satisfied." Jesus ESV Matthew 5:6 Chapter 30

- "Love your enemies and pray for those who persecute you." Jesus ESV Matthew 5:44 Chapter 44

- "Do not be like them; for your father knows what you need before you ask him. Pray, then, in this way our father who is in heaven, Hallowed be Your name. Your kingdom come Your will be done. On earth as it is in heaven. Give us this day our daily bread and forgive us our debts as we also have forgiven our debtors. And do not lead us into temptation but deliver us from evil." Jesus NASB Matthew 6 8-13 Chapter 47

- For if you forgive others their transgressions, your heavenly father will also forgive you. But if you do not forgive others, then your father will not forgive your transgressions. Jesus ESV Matthew 6:14-15 Chapter 47

- "No one can serve two masters; for either he will hate the one and love the other; or he will be devoted to one and despise the other. You cannot serve God and wealth." Jesus NASB Matthew 6:24 Chapter 45

- "Do not worry about tomorrow; for tomorrow will care for itself. Each day has enough trouble of its own." Jesus NASB Matthew 6:34 Chapter 77

- Do not judge so that you will not be judged. For in the way you judge, you will be judged; and by your standard of measure, it will be measured to you. Why do you look at the speck that is in your brother's eye, but do not notice the log that is in your own eye? Or how can you say to your brother, let me take the speck out of your eye, and behold, the log is in your own eye? You hypocrite, first take the log out of your own eye, and then you will see clearly to take the speck out of your brother's eye. Jesus NASB Matthew 7:1-5 Chapter 106

- "If you then, who are evil, know how to give good gifts to your children, how much more will your Father who is in heaven give good things to those who ask him! So whatever you wish that others would do to you, do also to them, for this is the law and the prophets." Jesus ESV Matthew 7:11- 12 Chapter 95

- In everything, treat people the same way you want them to treat you. Jesus NASB Matthew 7:12 Chapter 106

- "Enter by the narrow gate. For the gate is wide and the way is easy that leads to destruction, and those who enter by it are many. For the gate is narrow and the way is hard that leads to life, and those who find it are few." Jesus ESV Matthew 7:13-14 Chapter 51

- "Everyone who hears these words of mine and acts on them may be compared to a wise man who built his house on the rock. And the rain fell, and the floods came, and the winds blew and slammed against that house; and yet it did not fall for it had been founded on the rock. Everyone who hears these words of mine and does not act on them will be like a foolish man who built his house on the sand. The rain fell and the floods came and the winds blew and slammed against that house; and it fell-and great was its fall." Jesus NASB Matthew 7:24-27 Chapter 4 & 109

- "It is not those who are healthy who need a physician, but those who are sick. But go and learn what this means I desire compassion, and not sacrifice, for I did not come to call the righteous, but sinners." Jesus Matthew 9:12-13 Chapter 96

- Now when John heard in prison about the deeds of Christ, he sent word by his disciples and said to him, "Are you the one who is to come, or shall we look for another?" And Jesus answered them," Go and tell John what you hear and see the blind received their sight and the lame walk, lepers are cleansed and the deaf hear, and the dead are raised up, and the poor have good news preached to them. And blessed is the one who is not offended by me." ESV Matthew 11:2-6 Chapter 6

- "Come to Me, all who are weary and heavy-laden, and I will give you rest. Take My yoke upon you and learn from Me, for I am gentle and humble in heart, and you will find rest for your souls. For My yoke is easy and My burden is light." Jesus NASB Matthew 11:28-30 Chapter 61

- Peter said to Him, "Lord, if it is You, command me to come to You on the water." And He said, "Come!" And Peter got out of the boat, and walked on the water and came toward Jesus. But seeing the wind, he became frightened, and beginning to sink, he cried out, "Lord save me!" Immediately Jesus stretched out his hand and took hold of him and said to him "You of little faith, why did you doubt?" NASB Matthew 14:28-31 Chapter 39

- "This people honors me with their lips, but their heart is far from me; in vain do they worship me, teaching as doctrines the commandments of men." Jesus ESV Matthew 15:8-9. Chapter 11

- "Whoever then humbles himself as this child, he is the greatest in the kingdom of heaven." Jesus NASB Matthew 18:4 Chapter 19 & 55

- "The last shall be first, and the first last." Jesus NASB Matthew 20:16 Chapter 108

- "Render to Caesar the things that are Caesar's, and to God the things that are God's." Jesus ESV Matthew 22:21 Chapter 59 & 68

- "You shall love your neighbor as yourself." Jesus ESV Matthew 22:39 Chapter 67

- "You shall love the Lord your God with all your heart and with all your soul and with all your mind. This is the great and first Commandment. And a second is like it You shall Love your neighbor as yourself." Jesus ESV Matthew 22:37-39 Chapter 27

- That evening at sundown they brought to him all who were sick or oppressed by demons. And the whole city was gathered together at the door. And he healed many who were sick with various diseases, and cast out many demons. And he would not permit the demons to speak, because they knew him. ESV Mark 1:32-34 Chapter 49

- Then he went home, and the crowd gathered again, so that they could not even eat. And when his family heard it, they went out to seize him, for they were saying, "He is out of his mind." ESV Mark 3:20-21 Chapter 43 & 85

- They laughed at him. But he put them all outside and took the child's father and mother and those who were with him and went in where the child was. ESV Mark 4:40 Chapter 93

- And when Jesus had stepped out of the boat, immediately there met him out of the tombs a man with an unclean spirit. He lived among the tombs. And no one could bind him anymore, not even with a chain, for he had often been bound with shackles and chains, he wrenched the chains apart, and he broke the shackles in pieces. No one had the strength to subdue him. Night and day among the tombs and on the mountains he was always crying out and cutting himself with stones. And when he saw Jesus from afar, he ran and fell down before him. And crying out with a loud voice, he said," what have you to do with me, Jesus, son of the most high God? I adjure you by God, do not torment me." For he was saying to him," come out of the man, you unclean spirit!" And Jesus asked him," what is your name?" He replied," my name is Legion for we are many. ESV Mark 5 2-9 Chapter 37

- There was a woman who had had a discharge of blood for 12 years, and who had suffered much under many physicians, and had spent all that she had, and was no better but rather grew worse. ESV Mark 5:25-26 Chapter 26

- And the king said to the girl, "Ask me for whatever you wish, and I will give it to you." And he vowed to her, "Whatever you ask me, I will give you, up to half my kingdom." And she went out and said to her mother, "For what should I ask?" And she said, "The head of John the Baptist." And she came in immediately with haste to the king and asked, saying, "I want you to give me at once the head of John the Baptist on a platter." And the king was exceedingly sorry, but because of his oaths and his guests he did not want to break his word to her. ESV Mark 6:22- 26 Chapter 102

- "If anyone would come after me, let him deny himself and take up his cross and follow me. For whoever would save his life will lose it, but whoever loses his life for my sake and the gospel's will save it. For what does it profit a man to gain the whole world and forfeit his soul? For what can a man give in return for his soul? For whoever is ashamed of me and of my words in this adulterous and sinful generation, of him will the son of man also be ashamed when he comes in the glory of his father with the holy angels." Jesus ESV Mark 8:34-38 Chapter 110

- "If anyone would be first, he must be last of all and servant of all." Jesus ESV Mark 9:35 Chapter 108

- "Anyone who will not receive the kingdom of god like a little child will never enter it." Jesus NIV Mark 10:15 Chapter 19

- "No one is good except God alone." Jesus NASB Mark 10:18 Chapter 86

- "How difficult it will be for those who have wealth to enter the kingdom of God!" Jesus ESV Mark 10:23 Chapter 80

- "You know that those who are considered rulers of the Gentiles lord it over them, and their great ones exercise authority over them. But it shall not be so among you. But whoever would be great among you must be your servant, and whoever would be first among you must be slave of all. For even the Son of Man came not to be served but to serve, and to give his life as a ransom for many." Jesus ESV Mark 10:42-45 Chapter 16

- "Treat others the same way you want them to treat you." Jesus NASB Luke 6:31 Chapter 59

- A blind man cannot guide a blind man, can he? Will they not both fall into a pit? A pupil is not above his teacher; but everyone, after he has been fully trained, will be like his teacher. Jesus NASB Luke 6:39-40 Chapter 15

- Why do you look at the spec that is in your brothers' eye, but do not notice the log that is in your own eye? Or how can you say to your brother, brother, let me take out the spec that is in your eye, when you yourself do not see the log that is in your own eye? You hypocrite first take the log out of your own eye, and then you will see clearly to take out the spec that is in your brothers' eye. Jesus NASB Luke 6:41-42 Chapter 15

- "My brothers are these who hear the word of God and do it" Jesus NASB Luke 8:21 Chapter 9

- "Truly ,Truly, I say to you, unless one is born again he cannot see the kingdom of God." Jesus NASB John 3:3 Chapter 32

- "That which is born of the flesh is flesh, and that which is born of the spirit is spirit. Do not be amazed that I said to you, you must be born again. The wind blows where it wishes and you hear the sound of it, but do not know where it comes from and where it is going; so is everyone who is born of the Spirit?" Jesus NASB John 3:6-8 Chapter 76

- "Do not marvel that I said to you, you must be born again. The wind blows where it wishes, and you hear its sound, but you do not know where comes from or where it goes. So it is with everyone who is born of the spirit." Jesus ESV John 3:7-8 Chapter 33

- "God is Spirit, and those who worship him must worship in spirit and truth." Jesus ESV John 4:24 Chapter 97

- When Jesus saw him lying there, and knew that he had already been a long time in that condition, He said to him, "Do you wish to get well?" Jesus NASB John 5:6 Chapter 28

- "How can you believe, when you receive glory from one another and do not seek the glory that comes from the only God?" Jesus ESV John 5:44 Chapter 103

- Perceiving then that they were about to come and take him by force to make him king, Jesus withdrew again to the mountain by himself. ESV John 6:15 Chapter 84

- When they had rowed about three or 4 miles, they saw Jesus walking on the sea and coming near the boat, and they were frightened. But he said to them, "It is I, do not be afraid." Then they were glad to take him into the boat, and immediately the boat was at the land to which they were going. ESV John 6:19-21 Chapter 38

- "I am the bread of life; whoever comes to Me will not hunger, and whoever believes in Me will never thirst." Jesus NASB John 6:35 Chapter 30

- "If anyone is thirsty, let him come to Me and drink. He who believes in Me, as the Scripture said, from his innermost being will flow rivers of living water." Jesus NASB John 7:37- 38 Chapter 81

- "I am the light of the world. Whoever follows me will not walk in darkness, but will have the light of life." Jesus ESV John 8:12 Chapter 31

- "If you continue in my word, then you are truly disciples of Mine; and you will know the truth, and the truth will make you free." Jesus NASB John 8:31 Chapter 17

- "You Will know the truth, and the truth will make you free". Jesus NASB John 8:32 Chapter 97

- "I do not seek my own glory; there is One who seeks it, and he is the judge" Jesus ESV John 8:50 Chapter 91

- "Rabbi who sinned, this man or his parents, that he was born blind?" Jesus answered," It was not that this man sinned, or his parents, but that the works of God might be displayed in him." ESV John 9:2-3 Chapter 49

- I am the door; if anyone enters through Me; he will be saved, and will go in and out and find pasture. Jesus NASB John 10:9 Chapter 40

- "I am the good Shepherd. The good

Shepherd lays down his life for the sheep." Jesus ESV John 10:11. Chapter. 14

- "I am the good Shepherd. I know my own and my own know me," Jesus ESV John 10-14. Chapter 14

- "I lay down my life so that I may take it up again. No one has taken it away from Me, but I lay it down on My own initiative, I have authority to lay it down, and I have authority to take it up again. This commandment I received from my father." Jesus NASB John 10:17-18 Chapter 92

- "I told you, and you do not believe; the works that I do in My Father's name, these testify of Me. But you do not believe because you are not of My sheep. My sheep hear My voice, and I know them, and they follow me, and I give eternal life to them, and they will never perish; and no one will snatch them out of my hand. My Father, who has given them to me, is greater than all; and no one is able to snatch them out of the Father's hand. I and the father are one." Jesus NASB John 10:25-30 Chapter 37 & 62

- "I am the resurrection and the life; he who believes in Me will live even if he dies, and everyone who lives and believes in Me will never die. Do you believe this?" Jesus NASB John 11:25- 26 Chapter 29 & 65

- "If anyone serves me, he must follow me; and where I am, there will my servant be also. If anyone serves me, the father will honor him. " Jesus ESV John 12:26 Chapter 91

- "I am the way, and the truth, and the life; no one comes to the Father but through me. Jesus NASB John 14:6 Chapter 21 & 34 & 97

- "If you abide in Me, and My words abide in you, ask whatever you wish, and it will be done for you. My Father is glorified by this, that you bear much fruit, and so prove to be My disciples." Jesus NASB John 15:7-8 Chapter 78

- Then Simon Peter, having a sword, drew it and struck the high priest's servant and cut off his right ear. So Jesus said to Peter," Put your sword into its sheath; shall I not drink the cup that the father has given me. ESV John 18:10-11 Chapter 100

- For I am not ashamed of the gospel, for it is the power of God For salvation to everyone who believes. ESV Romans 1:16 Chapter 75

- What can be known about God is plain to them, because God has shown it to them. For his invisible attributes, namely, his eternal power and divine nature, have been clearly perceived, ever since the creation of the world, and the things that have been made. So they are without excuse. ESV Romans 1 19-20 Chapter 50

- For all have sinned and fall short of the glory of God, being justified as a gift by His grace through the redemption which is in Christ Jesus. NASB Romans 3:23-24 Chapter 8 & 52

- I am of the flesh, sold under sin. For I do not understand my own actions. For I do not do what I want, but I do the very thing I hate. ESV Romans 7:14- 15 Chapter 67

- Anyone who does not have the Spirit of Christ does not belong to him. But if Christ is in you, although the body is dead because of sin, the Spirit is life because of righteousness. If the spirit of him who raised Jesus from the dead dwells in you, he who raised Christ Jesus from the dead will also give life to your mortal bodies through his Spirit who dwells in you. ESV Romans 8:10-11 Chapter 18

- God causes all things to work together for good for those who love

God, to those who are called according to his purpose. NASB Romans 8:28 Chapter 1

- I say to everyone among you not to think more highly of himself than he ought to think; but to think so as to have sound judgment, as God has allotted to each a measure of faith. For just as we have many members in one body and all the members do not have the same function, so we, who are many, are one body in Christ, and individually members of one another. Since we have gifts that differ according to the grace given to us, each of us is to exercise them accordingly. NASB Romans 12:3-6 Chapter 16

- For you were called to freedom, brothers. Only do not use your freedom as an opportunity for the flesh, but through love serve one another. For the whole law is fulfilled in one word "You shall love your neighbor as yourself." But if you bite and devour one another, watch out that you are not consumed by one another. But I say, walk by the Spirit, and you will not gratify the desires of the flesh. For the desires of the flesh are against the spirit, and the desires of the Spirit are against the flesh, for these are opposed to each other, to keep you from doing the things you want to do. But if you are led by the spirit you are not under the law. Now the works of the flesh are evident sexual immorality, impurity, sensuality, idolatry, sorcery, enmity, strife, jealousy, fits of anger, rivalries, dissensions, divisions, envy, drunkenness, orgies, and things like these. I warn you, as I warned you before, that those who do such things will not inherit the kingdom of God. But the fruit of the Spirit is love, Joy, peace, patience, kindness, goodness, faithfulness, gentleness, self-control; against such things there is no law. And those who belong to Christ Jesus have crucified the flesh with its passions and desires. If we live by the Spirit, let us also keep in step with the Spirit. Let us not become conceited, provoking one another, envying one another. ESV Galatians 5:13-25 Chapter 105

- The fruit of the spirit is love, Joy, peace, patience, kindness, goodness, faithfulness, gentleness, self-control; against such things there is no law. NASB Galatians 5:22-23 Chapter 67 & 90

- By grace you have been saved through faith; and that not of yourselves, it is the gift of God; not as a result of works, so that no one may boast. NASB Ephesians 2 8-9 Chapter 63 & 66 & 99

- Be careful how you walk, not as unwise men but as wise, making the most of your time, because the days are evil. NASB Ephesians 5 15-16 Chapter 25

- Take the helmet of salvation, and the sword of the Spirit, which is the word of God, praying at all times in the spirit, with all prayer and supplication.

- To that end, keep alert with all perseverance. ESV Ephesians 6:17-18 Chapter 23

- And take the helmet of salvation, and the sword of the Spirit, which is the word of God. NASB Ephesians 6:17 Chapter 41

- "For our struggle is not against flesh and blood, but against the rulers, against the powers, against the world forces of this darkness, against the spiritual forces of wickedness in the heavenly places." Apostle Paul NASB Ephesians 6:12 Chapter 3 & 12 & 41

- For we are the circumcision; who worship by the Spirit of God and glory in Christ Jesus and put no confidence in the flesh. ESV Philippians 3:3 Chapter 64

- Forgetting what lies behind and straining forward to what lies ahead, I press on toward the goal for the prize of the upward call of God in Christ Jesus. Let those of us who are mature think this way, and if in anything you think otherwise, God will reveal that also to you. ESV Philippians 3:13 Chapter 53

- I do not consider that I have made it my own. But one thing I do forgetting what lies behind and straining forward to what lies ahead, I press on toward the goal for the prize of the upward call of God in Christ Jesus. Let those of us who are mature think this way, and if in anything you think otherwise, god will reveal that also to you. ESV Philippians 3:13-16 Chapter 107

- Be anxious for nothing, but in every-thing by prayer and supplication with thanksgiving let your requests be made known to God. And the peace of God, which surpasses all compre-hension, will guard your hearts and your minds in Christ Jesus. NASB Philippians 4:6-7 Chapter 7

- Whatever is true, whatever is hon-orable, whatever is just, whatever is pure, whatever is lovely, whatever is commendable, if there is any excel-lence, if there is anything worthy of praise, think about these things. ESV Philippians 4:8 Chapter 10

- I have learned to be content in what-ever circumstances I am. I know how to get along with humble means, and I also know how to live in prosper-ity; in any and every circumstance I have learned the secret of being filled and going hungry, both of hav-ing abundance and suffering need. I can do all things through him who strengthens me. NASB Philippians 4:11-13 Chapter 101

- I can do all things through him who strengthens me. NASB Philippians 4:13 Chapter 64 & 87

- God willed to make known what is the riches of the glory of this mystery among the Gentiles, which is Christ in you, the hope of glory. NASB Colossians 1:27 Chapter 18 & 90

- God made alive together with him, having forgiven us all our trespasses, by canceling the record of debt that stood against us with its legal demands. This he set aside, nailing it to the cross. He disarmed the rulers and the authorities and put them to open shame, by triumphing over them in him. Therefore let no one pass judgment on you in questions of food and drink, or with regard to a festival or a new moon or a Sabbath. These are a shadow of the things to come, but the substance belongs to Christ. Let no one disqualify you, insisting on asceticism and worship of angels, going on in detail about visions, puffed up without reason by his sensuous mind, and not holding fast to the Head, from whom the whole body, nourished and knit together through its joints and ligaments, grows with the growth that is from God. If with Christ you died to the elemental spirits of the world, why, as if you were still alive in the world, do you submit to regulations-Do not handle, Do not taste, Do not touch(referring to things that all perish as they are used)-according to human precepts and teachings? These have indeed an appearance of wisdom in promoting self-made religion and asceticism and severity to the body, but they are of no value in stopping the indulgence of the flesh. ESV Colossians 2:13-23. Chapter 11

- See that you fulfill the ministry that you have received in the Lord. ESV Colossians 4:17 Chapter 83

- We wanted to come to you-I, Paul, again and again-but Satan hindered us. ESV 1 Thessalonians 2:18 Chapter 60

- Let us be sober, having put on the breast plate of faith and love, and as a helmet, the hope of salvation. NASB 1 Thessalonians 5:8 Chapter 48

- See that no one repays anyone evil for evil, but always seek to do good to one another and to everyone. Rejoice always; pray without ceasing; give thanks in all circumstances; for this is the will of God in Christ Jesus for you. Do not quench the spirit. ESV 1 Thessalonians 5:15-19 Chapter 44 & 56

- With all wicked deception for those who are perishing, because they refused to love the truth and So

be saved. ESV 2 Thessalonians 2:10
Chapter 94

- We also once were foolish ourselves,
disobedient, deceived, enslaved to
various lusts and pleasures, spending our life in malice and envy, hateful, hating one another. But when the
kindness of God our Savior and His
love for mankind appeared, He saved
us, not on the basis of deeds which
we have done in righteousness, but
according to his mercy, by the washing of regeneration and renewing by
the Holy Spirit, whom he poured out
upon us richly through Jesus Christ
our Savior, so that being justified by
his grace we would be made heirs
according to the hope of eternal life.
NASB Titus 3:3-7 Chapter 82

- You have come to need milk and not
solid food. For everyone who partakes
only of milk is not accustomed to the
word of righteousness, for he is an in-

fant. But solid food is for the mature, who because of practice have their senses trained to discern Good and Evil. NASB Hebrews 5:12-14 Chapter 22

- Therefore, since we have so great a cloud of witnesses surrounding us, let us also lay aside every encumbrance and the sin which so easily in tangles us, and let us run with endurance the race that is set before us, fixing our eyes on Jesus, the author and perfecter of faith, who for the joy set before him endured the cross, despising the shame and has sat down at the right-hand of the throne of God. NASB Hebrews 12:1-2 Chapter 69 & 75 & 104

- Do not neglect to show hospitality to strangers, for by this some have entertained angels without knowing it. NASB Hebrews 13:1-2 Chapter 73

- Count it all joy, my brothers, when you meet trials of various kinds, for you know that the testing of your faith produces steadfastness. And let steadfastness have its full effect, that you may be perfect and complete, lacking in nothing. ESV James 1:2-4 Chapter 57

- If any of you lacks wisdom, let him ask God, who gives generously to all without reproach, and it will be given him. But let him ask in faith, with no doubting, for the one who doubts is like a wave of the sea that is driven and tossed by the wind. For that person must not suppose that he will receive anything from the Lord; he is a double minded man, unstable in all his ways. ESV James 1:5-8 Chapter20

- The brother of humble circumstances is to glory in his high position; and the rich man is to glory in his humiliation. NASB James 1:9-10 Chapter 80

- Show me your faith apart from your works, and I will show you my faith by my works. You believe that God is one; you do well. Even the demons believe- and shutter! Do you want to be shown, you foolish person, that faith apart from works is useless? ESV James 2:18-20 Chapter 79

- No one can tame the tongue; it is a restless evil and full of deadly poison. NASB James 3:8 Chapter 98

- Does a fountain send out from the same opening both fresh and bitter water? NASB James 3:11 Chapter 98

- The wisdom from above is first pure, then peaceable, gentle, reasonable, full of mercy and good fruits, unwavering without hypocrisy. NASB James 3:17 Chapter 20

- God opposes the proud but gives grace to the humble. ESV James 4:6 Chapter 55

- God opposes the proud but gives grace to the humble. Submit yourselves therefore to God. Resist the devil, and he will flee from you. Draw near to God, and he will draw near to you. Cleanse your hands you sinners, and purify your hearts, you double minded. ESV James 4:6-8 Chapter 10

- God opposes the proud but gives grace to the humble. Submit yourselves therefore to God. Resist the devil, and he will flee from you. Draw near to God, and he will draw near to you. Cleanse your hands you sinners, and purify your hearts, you double minded.

- Be wretched and mourn and weep. Let your laughter be turned into mourning and your joy to gloom. Humble yourselves before the Lord, and he will exalt you. ESV James 4 6-9 Chapter 13

- Come now, you who say," Today or tomorrow we will go into such and such a town and spend a year there and trade and make a profit"-yet you do not know what tomorrow will bring. What is your life? For you are a mist that appears for a little time and then vanishes. Instead you ought to say. "If the Lord wills, we will live and do this or that." As it is, you boast in your arrogance. All such boasting is evil. ESV James 4:13-16 Chapter 88

- Putting aside all malice and all deceit and hypocrisy and envy and all slander, like newborn babies, long for the pure milk of the word, so that by it you may grow in respect to salvation, if you have tasted the kindness of the Lord. NASB 1 Peter 2:1-3 Chapter 22

- Dear friends, I urge you, as foreigners and exiles, to abstain from sinful desires, which wage war against your soul. NIV 1 Peter 2:11 Chapter74

- He himself bore our sins in His body on the cross, so that we might die to sin and live to righteousness; for by his wounds you were healed. NASB 1 Peter 2:24 Chapter 63

- Christ also died for sins once for all, the just for the unjust, so that he might bring us to God, having been put to death in the flesh, but made alive in the spirit. NASB 1 Peter 3:18 Chapter 71

- Humble yourselves under the mighty hand of God, that he may exalt you at the proper time, casting all your anxiety on Him, because He cares for you. Be of sober spirit, be on the alert. Your adversary, the devil, prowls around like a roaring lion, seeking someone to devour. But resist him, firm in your faith, knowing that the same experiences of suffering are being accomplished by your brethren who are in the world. After you have suffered for a little while, the God of all grace, who called you to His eternal glory in Christ, will Himself perfect, confirm, strengthen and establish you. To him be dominion forever and ever. Amen NASB 1 Peter 5:6-11 Chapter 46

- They promised them freedom, but they themselves are slaves of corruption. For whatever overcomes a person, to that he is enslaved. ESV 2 Peter 2:19 Chapter 5

- If we confess our sins, he is faithful and just to forgive us our sins and to cleanse us from all unrighteousness. ESV 1 John 1:9 Chapter 71

- Building yourselves up in your most holy faith and praying in the Holy Spirit keep yourselves in the love of God, waiting for the mercy of our Lord Jesus Christ that leads to eternal life. And have mercy on those who doubt; save others by snatching them out of the fire; to others show mercy with fear, hating even the garment stained by the flesh. ESV Jude:20-23 Chapter 83

Appendix 2

- Happy Warriors are asumption-cautious. Chapter 2

- Happy Warriors know themselves and their enemy. Chapter 3 & 12

- Happy Warriors have the perfect foundation. Chapter 4 & 109

- Happy Warriors are free everywhere. Chapter 5

- Happy Warriors enjoy their freedom. Chapter 6

- Happy Warriors pray. Chapter 7

- Happy Warriors are unique. Chapter 8 & 43 & 85

- Happy Warriors know who they are. Chapter 9

- Happy Warriors control their thoughts. Chapter 10

- Happy Warriors are not religious. Chapter 11

- Happy Warriors respect the chain of command. Chapter 13

- Happy Warriors are careful who they follow. Chapter 14

- Happy Warriors have excellent vision. Chapter 15

- Happy Warriors know who they are. Chapter 16

- Happy Warriors walk in truth. Chapters 17

- Happy Warriors embrace mystery. Chapter 18

- Happy Warriors are humble. Chapter 19

- Happy Warriors seek wisdom. Chapter 20

- Happy Warriors know the way. Chapter 21

- Happy Warriors know what's good for them. Chapter 22

- Happy Warriors fight. Chapter 23

- Happy Warriors seek knowledge and wisdom. Chapter 24

- Happy Warriors are cautious.
  Chapter 25

- Happy Warriors are careful who
  they trust. Chapter 26

- Happy Warriors love themselves.
  Chapter 27

- Happy Warriors want to be well.
  Chapter 28

- Happy Warriors are teachable.
  Chapter 29 & 35

- Happy Warriors eat and drink well.
  Chapter 30

- Happy Warriors use all the weapons
  of war. Chapter 31

- Happy Warriors know what it takes
  to see. Chapter 32

- Happy Warriors know how to look.
  Chapter 33

- Happy Warriors value training.
  Chapter 36

- Happy Warriors know who to listen
  to. Chapter 37

- Happy Warriors focus on Jesus. Chapter 38 & 39 & 53

- Happy Warriors use the door. Chapter 40

- Happy Warriors use their weapons. Chapter 41

- Happy Warriors are no better than anybody else. Chapter 42

- Happy Warriors do not cut themselves. Chapter 44

- Happy Warriors serve their commander. Chapter 45

- Happy Warriors know their limitations. Chapter 46

- Happy Warriors forgive themselves and others. Chapter 47

- Happy Warriors hope. Chapter 48

- Happy Warriors make good choices … but still suffer. Chapter 49

- Happy Warriors search for the truth. Chapter 50 & 54

- Happy Warriors use the narrow gate. Chapter 51

- Happy Warriors give grace to themselves and others. Chapter 52

- Happy Warriors are humble. Chapter 55

- Happy Warriors are thankful. Chapter 56

- Happy Warriors value training. Chapter 57

- Happy Warriors are chemical-cautious. Chapter 58 & 105

- Happy Warriors show respect. Chapter 59

- Happy Warriors know that life is not fair. Chapter 60

- Happy Warriors team up well. Chapter 61

- Happy Warriors feel secure. Chapter 62

- Happy Warriors know what Jesus did for them. Chapter 63

- Happy Warriors ask for help. Chapter 64 & 78 & 87

- Happy Warriors look forward to going home. Chapter 65

- Happy Warriors give grace to themselves and others. Chapter 66

- Happy Warriors love themselves. Chapter 67

- Happy Warriors follow the rules. Chapter 68

- Happy Warriors focus. Chapter 69

- Happy Warriors don't try to do everything themselves. Chapter 70

- Happy Warriors respond appropriately to all voices. Chapter 71

- Happy Warriors listen to the one who loves them. Chapter 72

- Happy Warriors are careful with the assumptions. Chapter 73

- Happy Warriors control themselves. Chapter 74

- Happy Warriors point to Jesus when shamed. Chapter 75

- Happy Warriors train their senses. Chapter 76

- Happy Warriors are content.
  Chapter 77 & 101

- Happy Warriors act on truth.
  Chapter 79

- Happy Warriors are wealthy.
  Chapter 80

- Happy Warriors are skilled in the
  use of all weapons. Chapter 81

- Happy Warriors are not foolish.
  Chapter 82

- Happy Warriors know their mission.
  Chapter 83

- Happy Warriors have their own
  agenda. Chapter 84

- Happy Warriors understand no one
  is perfect. Chapter 86

- Happy Warriors are flexible.
  Chapter 88

- Happy Warriors trust their commanding officer. Chapter 89

- Happy Warriors have excellent self-
  control. Chapter 90

- Happy Warriors do not glorify themselves. Chapter 91

- Happy Warriors are powerful. Chapter 92

- Happy Warriors ignore the critics. Chapter 93

- Happy Warriors love the truth. Chapter 94

- Happy Warriors control themselves. Chapter 95

- Happy Warriors never give up. Chapter 96

- Happy Warriors value the truth. Chapter 97

- Happy Warriors are word-cautious. Chapter 98

- Happy Warriors take nothing for granted. Chapter 99

- Happy Warriors are weapons-cautious. Chapter 100

- Happy Warriors are content. Chapter 101

- Happy Warriors are promise-careful. Chapter 102

- Happy Warriors value glory. Chapter 103

- Happy Warriors compete to win. Chapter 104

- Happy Warriors are chemical-cautious. Chapter 105

- Happy Warriors are not always heroes. Chapter 106

- Happy Warriors do not focus on the past. Chapter 107

- Happy Warriors are successful. Chapter 108

- Happy Warriors have the perfect foundation. Chapter 109

- Happy Warriors understand that our time here on planet Earth is tiny compared to eternity. Chapter 110